Ten Woodstock Families of the
Sixteenth and Seventeenth Centuries

Pat Crutch

Mary Hodges.

Ten Woodstock Families

of the Sixteenth and

Seventeenth Centuries

Patricia Crutch

Foreword by Mary Hodges

THE WYCHWOOD PRESS *FOR*
THE WOODSTOCK SOCIETY LOCAL HISTORY GROUP

Wychwood Press books may be ordered from bookshops or (post free) from Jon Carpenter Publishing, Alder House, Market Street, Charlbury, OX7 3PH
01608 811969

e-mail: wychwood@joncarpenter.co.uk

Credit card orders should be phoned or faxed to 01689 870437 or 01608 811969

First published in 2005 by
The Wychwood Press
an imprint of Jon Carpenter Publishing
Alder House, Market Street, Charlbury, Oxfordshire OX7 3PH

ISBN 1 902279 22 0

Printed in England by Antony Rowe Ltd., Eastbourne

Contents

Acknowledgements

These family studies have developed as a result of work undertaken since the mid 1980's by the Woodstock Society's local history group with Miss Mary Hodges as tutor.

Thanks are due to all the members of the Local History Group for their much needed advice and encouragement. Thanks especially to our leader Mary Hodges who has written the foreword to the study. Royston Taylor gave valuable guidance on content of the text and Joan Walsh undertook early proof reading. Former member Jack Shipp provided further information on the Whitton family.

Thanks to John Allen for information and drawings of the coats of arms of Fletcher and Whitton families.

By courtesy of the Mayor and Council Dr. Molly Barratt, the honorary archivist for Woodstock, provided copies of the documents studied.

The Oxfordshire Museum at Woodstock provides a meeting room for the group and West Oxfordshire District Council gave financial support for room rental. Staff and volunteers at the Museum Learning Centre have given help and advice with computers.

The Bodleian Library, Centre for Oxfordshire Studies and Oxford Record Office have allowed reproduction of photographs and documents in their collections.

Locally, Brenda Cripps gave permission to reproduce her design for the Woodstock Broderers' Wallhanging used on the front cover. Robert Pomfret added improvements to the design of the parish map.

The Marc Fitch fund gave a grant towards publication costs.

Abbreviations

Aston	TH Aston, (ed.), *History of the University of Oxford* iii (1986).
Ballard	A Ballard, *Chronicles of Woodstock* (1896).
Chambers	EK Chambers, *Sir Henry Lee, an Elizabethan Portrait* (1936).
Clerus	Canon Oldfield's index to Oxfordshire clergy (in ORO).
Collins	Collins English Dictionary
Corbett	E Corbett, *History of Spelsbury* (1962).
Cox	J and N Cox, *"Probate 1500 –1800"* in T.Arkell, N.Evans & N.Goose, eds. *When Death Do Us Part* (Local Population Studies - Oxford 2000).
Eddershaw	D Eddershaw, *The Civil War in Oxfordshire*, Oxfordshire Books, (1995).
Grundon	I Grundon, *Fletchers House, Woodstock: An Architectural and Historical Analysis* Oxoniensia LXV (2000).
Hodges	Mary Hodges, unpublished paper on Owen Fletcher, recusant.
Houlbrooke	RA Houlbrooke, *The English Family 1450 – 1700* (1986).
Howard-Drake	J Howard-Drake, *Calendars of Oxford Church Court Depositions* (Oxford 1991-98).
Howard Gray	Howard Gray, *English Field Systems*, (1915).
Huxford	J Huxford, *Coats of arms of Sussex Families* (1982).
Jones	J Jones, *Balliol College, A History* (1988).
MSS Wills	Oxon Wills & Inventories of the Oxford Diocese (in ORO). See Appendix.
Marshall	E Marshall, *Early History of Woodstock Manor & its Environs* (1873).
Norwood	RP Norwood, *History of Kiddington,*(1934).
OED	Oxford English Dictionary.
OHS	*Oxfordshire Historical Society*.
ORO	Oxfordshire Record Office.
ORS	*Oxfordshire Record Society*.
PRO PROB 11	Wills in Public Record Office (now National Archives). See Appendix.
Shipp	J Shipp, *The Whitton family of Woodstock Park* (unpublished).
Slack	P Slack, 'Books of orders'. The making of English social policy 1577-1631'. *Transactions of the Royal Historical Society* 5th series Vol.30 (1980).
Spufford	M Spufford , *"Religious Preambles…"* in T.Arkell, N.Evans & N.Goose, eds. *When Death Do Us Part* (Local Population Studies - Oxford 2000).

Taylor	RF Taylor, *Debts and Credits in Woodstock Probates 1533 to 1700* (unpublished).
VCH	*Victoria County History, Oxon* xii, ed A. Crossley, (Oxford 1990).
Walter	J Walter, *The Oxfordshire Rising,* Past & Present (1988)
Weinstock	MMB Weinstock , (ed.), *Hearth Tax Returns – Oxfordshire 1665* ORS Vol. 21, (1940).
WBM	Woodstock Borough Muniments B = Box number. See Appendix.
WBM	B78/2 Woodstock Borough Court Book 1607-14.
WBM	B78/3 Woodstock Borough Court Book 1614 -22.
WCA	M Maslen (ed.), *Woodstock Chamberlains' Accounts 1609-50*; ORS Vol.54, (1985).
WCBk	Taylor RF (ed.), *Calendar of the Court Books of the Borough of New Woodstock 1588-1595*; ORS Vol.63, (2002)

List of Illustrations

Foreword

Before the mid 1950s historians studied single families or elite families as part of their more general study of historical matters. The emergence of demographic studies and the work of the Annales school of history in France has brought the family into the main stream of historical studies. Demographers look for information about families as part of their work on populations, since the reconstitution of families, usually from parish registers, extends the reconstruction of populations over time. Social and economic history cannot be written without reference to the changing structures of families and this is especially true of the period from 1500 to 1800. For this period, if we are fortunate, we have in England the Parish Registers from which family reconstitution may be possible. From this source we may be able to see for what length of time a family group (indentified by the surname) persisted in a particular place. "Old families last not three oaks" said Sir Thomas Browne in the 17th century; "clogs to clogs in three generations" the proverb tells us. Does that matter? Communities small and large are made up of groups which we may call households. In some ways this is a more useful word for historians to use than family and is the word used by the 19th century census in collecting data from communities – it was the Head of Household who was asked to provide the information about each person. A household may contain those related by blood, and others – servants, friends, apprentices and so on. When Geoffrey King wrote his study of population in the 17th century he reckoned that a noble household might contain on average forty persons. Much work has been done by historians to find out how many people might be expected to be within a household in the centuries between 1500 and 1800. Parish Register data does not tell us this and few communities have other records from which information can come. We need to see the household as an economic and social unit from which the wider community derives its structure and purpose. Before the 19th century communities were dependent on the production of their needs from within a quite small geographical area. At the lowliest level people were engaged in food production, essential for their community. Animals provided transport, but most people walked and therefore markets – where items other than food could be bought – needed to be within walking distance for everyone. Market towns were organised so that no-one was more than 7 miles from the nearest market – it was considered possible to get to market and back in a day. Market towns provided opportunities to buy goods and many of these items were made in the market town.

Woodstock was founded in about 1170 by King Henry II whose royal palace stood in Woodstock Park; Blenheim Palace stands close to the site of this royal palace. Very soon people arrived to take up plots in the new town from which they could conduct businesses. The town prospered and in 1453 received a Royal Charter with a constitution for town government identical to the constitution of another Royal Borough, Windsor. By 1600 there were about 700 people in the town. Lists of occupations show anything from attorneys to wheelwrights. The town was governed by a Mayor and Corporation; it had its own Borough Court which met every other Monday. Here cases concerning the local community were heard and disputes about debt sorted out. The Borough owned property and had a considerable income from rents. It controlled the Market and the behaviour of people who came to the market.

For the men of Woodstock the pinnacle of ambition was to become a member of the Common Council and then to rise through the ranks of Borough offices to become Mayor. The Mayor and aldermen were Justices of the Peace also. The households and families which made up this inner group have left many records from which some reconstruction of their lives and work can be made. This information tells us much about the economic and social basis of Woodstock life in the period 1500 – 1700. The way in which households were related to one another can be seen and the role of marriage between family groups tells us how the bonds of society may have worked. These household and family ties could provide the financial backing needed to launch new business, to arrange apprenticeships and to lend money for new projects. At this time the role of men in the family was pre-eminent. The authority of the father was complete and wives and children were expected to obey him. He commanded his household also with servants and apprentices to be cared for. But the family studies in this book show that women were regarded as important partners in the life and development of the household. Since few marriages lasted beyond 25 years and, as today, men were more likely to die relatively young leaving a widow to carry on the family and household, the role of widows in particular was important. They were often left with young children to bring up, they might continue to run the family business, they might use their assets to lend money within their community.

In Woodstock we can still see some of the houses in which these people lived and the setting of streets and market place within which they lived their lives. The range of documents from which our information comes is wide, from Court Boooks to wills, inventories and Parish Registers. A full list of these sources appears as an appendix.

In this survey by Patricia Crutch of some of the prominent families all these sources have been used to produce histories of the families and to show how the families and households made Woodstock such an important and prosperous place.

Mary Hodges

Introduction

The town of Woodstock[1] was founded by Henry II in the mid-12th century on around 60 acres of waste ground bounded by the existing parishes of Wootton to the north, Bladon to the south and Hensington to the east. The western boundary comprised the royal park containing a lodge or manor used by the monarchs when hunting in the surrounding Wychwood forest.[2] Seemingly the king required his retinue to be housed closer to the manor than at the existing hamlet north of the Glyme and the two settlements became known as Old Woodstock and New Woodstock.

The medieval town was laid out around a large triangular market place. The lengthy burgage plots with narrow street frontages can be detected to the present day in property boundaries of Oxford Street, Market Street and High Street.[3] The town was allowed markets and fairs to provide employment and income for inhabitants in the royal absence. In 1453 Henry VI granted the town a charter, based upon that existing for royal Windsor; it was renewed by Charles II in 1664 at the restoration. Queen Elizabeth I granted the town a market for wool by charter of 1565.[4]

By the 16th and 17th centuries, the time of this study, the town's structure had altered with some central infilling to form the present day layout. On the town hall site was a market cross and to its east the guildhall, a location for council meetings and the fortnightly portmoot court. Several of the buildings around today's market place were notable inns where the

Initial letter of Queen Elizabeth's charter of 1565

king's entourage would lodge when he was in residence at the manor. In the early 17th century these central properties around the market place were prestigious addresses and mostly occupied by the town's aldermen.

Town government

The majority of these ten family stories chart the rise of one or more individuals to office in the town. The constitution of 1580 outlined their various duties:[5]

The *mayor*, elected annually in September, usually held office for two years. He sat as JP in the courts, acted as clerk to the market and presided at annual audits of churchwardens' and chamberlains' accounts. He entertained visitors to the town and was required to attend church services on holy days along with other councillors; it was his privilege to allot seating within the church. The mayor's annual salary was £10 and in addition he was entitled to certain fees from the courts and other 'perks' by way of expenses.

The mayor was chosen from the five borough *aldermen*.[6] As this office was conferred for life the arrangement blocked promotion for some residents worthy of the office. On the death of an alderman a common councillor was chosen to replace him; the constitution required the new alderman to have served as chamberlain. Aldermen always headed lists of councillors and inhabitants, signed official records of town business and were involved in economic management, sometimes lending money to the corporation.

The important office of *town clerk* was a salaried position. As clerk of court he arranged proceedings at the fortnightly portmoot court, attended Oxford assizes and liaised with the borough recorder in cases of dispute or legal complication. He arranged the collection of rents for the corporation's properties and kept the official records of property exchanges, chamberlains' accounts and acts of council.

Chamberlains usually served for two years being selected or re-elected at their annual audit in December after having served in the lesser offices of constable, tithingman and churchwarden. They accounted for receipts and expenses incurred in keeping the town clean and in good order and repair.

The post of *sergeant at mace* was conferred for life. He was required to carry the mace ahead of the mayor and councillors in procession; a ceremony performed to the present day. In the 16th and 17th centuries he had many more duties; licensing stallholders at market, appointing night watchmen to keep order in the town, maintaining the gaol and guarding prisoners; he also acted as attorney in the portmoot court and handled writs.

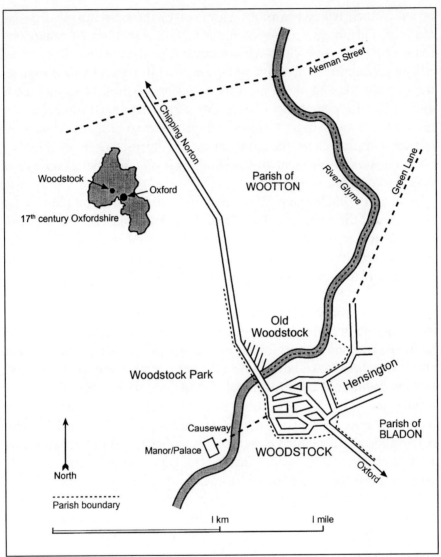

The position and layout of the town of Woodstock; showing boundaries of adjoining parishes.

Minor officers were elected at the Sessions of Peace and View of Frankpledge, held in April and October every year. The post of *constable* changed hands frequently; with responsibility for keeping law and order and with powers of arrest, this was perhaps the most hazardous of town offices. The two *aletasters* had more pleasant duties, but as well as testing the quality of ale brewed for sale in the town they were also responsible for other foodstuffs and checking weights and measures. By long established custom the four *tithingmen* were required to vouch for the good behaviour of ten of their fellow townsfolk. However, by the sixteenth century, the aletasters and tithingmen had become largely honorary titles. Appointments to the post of *surveyor of the highways* occur from time to time.

The constitution stated that only *freemen* of the town had the right to trade. They were admitted from the ranks of freemen's sons and town apprentices; the chamberlains' accounts record many such admissions. A man marrying a freeman's widow was also allowed his freedom as were outsiders or 'foreigners' the latter paying £5. Freemen were privileged to settle disputes for debts of five shillings or less before the mayor rather than through the courts.

A *rector* of Bladon and Woodstock was instituted from 1269 under patronage of the monarch.[7] There was also a *curate* and a *clerk to the church* probably appointed by him. At their annual audit in November two *church-wardens* were elected, one each by the minister and the mayor, along with *sidesmen* and *collectors* or *overseers of the poor.*

Following Henry VIII's dissolution of the monasteries the release of church property enabled gentry and yeoman classes to increase their land holdings. The king's agents for the Woodstock area, Leonard Chamberlain and Richard Andrews, both lived in the town. Father and son Owen and George Whitton, comptrollers of Woodstock park, acquired estates locally and leading townspeople such as alderman Thomas Fletcher purchased former chantry property within Woodstock and district. The corporation also benefitted from the release of chantry property and early 17th century rent rolls include income from chantry quit rents alongside rents for property granted to Woodstock by its charters.

In the last quarter of the 16th century there was much bad feeling between local gentry and town councillors.[8] Mayor William Skelton and alderman George Whitton quarrelled openly for control of the council and as a result Whitton was disfranchised but continued as member of parliament and local JP.

The 1590s were years of poor harvests and subsequent high mortality; unrest centred in the town when local yeomen claimed the situation had worsened after enclosures of land by the gentry, notably George Whitton and his associates. So great was the discontent that in 1596 an uprising was attempted.[9]

The first decade of the 17th century saw the demise of George Whitton and arrival of Edmund Hiorne as town clerk. These two events led to a period of stability in town government following the earlier discord among town councillors and local gentry. The chosen aldermen were well-established tradesmen with innkeepers and victuallers forming a large part of the council and this pattern continued throughout Hiorne's clerkship. Due to preservation of his careful records, the first half of the 17th century is the best-documented period of this study.

Royalist Edmund Hiorne was replaced by parliamentarian John Williams as town clerk during the civil war years; Williams' records survive but without the attention to detail practised by Hiorne. At the restoration the king's commissioners ousted Williams, with the mayor and around half of his council, and re-appointed Hiorne, by then an elderly man. The common council was reformed after 1662; Woodstock MP, Sir Littleton Osbaldeston, and other local gentry were sworn in as members and total control of the council again passed from resident townsmen. The next town clerk, George Ryves, husband of Hiorne's granddaughter, arrived in 1664 to be succeeded by his son, also named George Ryves, and the Ryves family guided the town into the 18th century.

Religion

In Tudor times frequent religious changes led to tension between those remaining in the Roman church and followers of the new Church of England. Will makers in early 16th century left their souls to God and the Blessed Virgin Mary and the Company of Heaven but later in that century wording of religious preambles changed, testators left their soul to Almighty God and his son Jesus Christ hoping for remission of their sins.[10] The church of St. Mary Magdalene in Woodstock saw the change from Roman to Church of England teachings during this time. In 1533 John Taylor left a pound of wax for lights before images of Ss. Mary, Margaret, George, Christopher, Clement and St. Roke. Chantry priests were resident in Woodstock until the late 16th century. One of these, Sir Martyn Cave (d.1571), took part in town affairs such as witnessing and overseeing of wills and perhaps tutoring the sons of local freemen.

It was the custom in the early 16th century to leave money for upkeep of the church building and to maintain lights on high altar, rood screen and porch. Later that century testators left small bequests of a few pence to Woodstock church and the mother church of Oxford. By early 17th century Woodstock had more puritan tendencies and bequests to the church for inauguration of sermons were usual; it became practice to invite clerics to preach on holy days. Leading townsfolk entertained these preachers who included William Laud, always referred to as 'Mr. Dr. Lawde' who preached before the King in the manor house chapel; he became Chancellor of Oxford University and Archbishop of Canterbury and held great power during Charles I's reign.

Nationally, in Tudor times terrible punishments and execution awaited those suspected of plotting against the throne to bring about religious conversion of the state. Woodstock with its royal residence might have been influenced by its closeness to the royal manor and visits by the monarchy, but there appears to have been little religious intolerance between inhabitants. Nevertheless the town produced one noted recusant, Owen Fletcher.[11] Under the Stuarts religious divisions eased to some extent but James I encouraged enquiries into witchcraft and at least one accusation was made against a Woodstock woman in his time.[12]

Royalty and parliament

King Henry VIII visited the town regularly for hunting in Woodstock park but Princess Elizabeth had been detained in the manor during her sister's reign and paid few visits to the town as queen. Her Champion, Sir Henry Lee, provided theatrical entertainments for her when she visited him at his lodge in 1572 and 1574.[13]

James I was often at Woodstock manor and enjoyed hunting in Wychwood as did Charles I from his civil war headquarters in Oxford. The king's presence here naturally attracted attention from Cromwell's army and the town saw the passage of regiments of both sides with the manor house changing hands several times. Woodstock, like many other towns, would have experienced much discomfort during the war years; armies required food, drink and lodging as they passed through but often brought disease with them and were unable to pay for their supplies.[14] Extensive damage was caused to the park by the civil war and under parliamentary rule royal estates were badly managed and much timber destroyed. Woodstock manor was not popular with the later Stuarts and suffered neglect making it almost uninhabitable. However, Col. Charles Fleetwood, Cromwell's son in law, followed by Lord Lovelace, resided in the patched up buildings. In 1676 Lovelace laid out a racecourse in the park, attracting visits from nobility and gentry thus bringing some tourist trade to Woodstock.

In the early 18th century Queen Anne presented the royal park and manor to John Churchill, Duke of Marlborough, in gratitude for his victory over the French at the battle of Blenheim. This brought to an end the town's close association with royalty and inevitably town government changed as the Marlborough's influenced the structure of the council.

The ten Woodstock families

It is reckoned that the span of any family within a locality is two or three generations in the male line and six of these ten families bear out the premise. Thomas *Bradshaw* and Thomas *Browne*, both very influential in town affairs, stayed for only two generations as did the *Bradshaw* family of mercers and the *Nashes* of Old Woodstock; the *Johnsons*, also mercers, are only traceable to two generations with any certainty. The *Fletcher* family however, aldermen from before 1545, stretched to over five generations declining in influence over the 17th century, whereas the innkeeping *Glover* family rose from shoemakers and bakers in mid-16th century to aldermen by 1610 and are traceable to six generations. The *Whittons* served for six generations as agents for the king and comptrollers of Woodstock park. The *Coopers*, yeomen, farmed in Hensington for about one hundred years from mid-16th to mid-17th centuries; with the aid of parish registers this family can be traced into the early 18th century and at least nine generations.

Woodstock borough muniments provide a range of documents for family studies:

The *Borough Constitution* of 1580 details the rules and regulations by which the town was governed.[15]

The *Portmoot Court* books record interaction between townspeople and outsiders over debts and disputes as well as property transactions by proclamation, indentures of apprenticeship and appointment of guardians. The meetings of the View of Frankpledge or court leet are also documented in the court books along with Sessions of the Peace, Assizes of Bread and Ale, Market Courts and enquiries into use of Flesh in Lent. From 1608 to 1613 these same books record criminal examinations by local JPs.[16]

Churchwardens' and *Chamberlains' accounts* record a few early burials and other family information. The chamberlains' accounts list expenses and disbursements, maintenance of the town's buildings and streets, admission of freemen, social problems and arrangements for care of less fortunate families.[17]

Leases and *Rent rolls* trace ownership of property through the generations.

Parish registers for New Woodstock date from 1653. Earlier registers, described in churchwardens' accounts of the 1630s, have not survived. The villages of Wootton, including Old Woodstock, and Bladon, including Hensington, have registers dating from the mid-16th century; in the earliest years, however, entries are sparse as only baptisms, marriages and burials of more prominent residents were registered.

Combined family tree showing intermarriages between foremost families of 16th and 17th century Woodstock

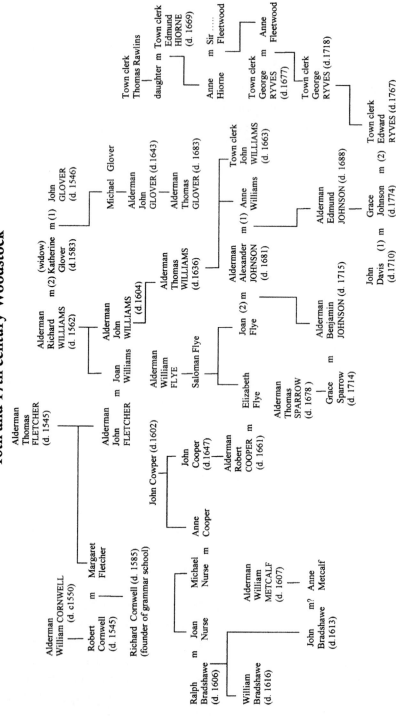

In the absence of parish registers, *probate documents* are vital for the study of family histories. Apart from a few wills proved in the Prerogative Court of Canterbury, Woodstock probate records date from 1530.[18] These allow reconstitution of local families more than a century before parish registers commence. This study includes information drawn from 70 Oxon wills and 12 PCC wills.[19]

Conclusion

Local history is about ordinary people and their everyday lives. This study aims to relate changing events affecting Woodstock families in the 16th and 17th centuries using the range of records available in local archives. Inevitably the more successful residents are best documented and, due to Edmund Hiorne's careful notes, the early 17th century contains most information on town affairs. Family history studies have revealed many links by marriage between Woodstock's 'ruling' families.[20] One or two families have been followed into the early 18th century where there is sufficient information in parish registers.

References

1   Old English 'a wooded place' or 'clearing in a wood'. OUP Oxford Names Index.
2   The building referred to throughout as Woodstock Manor was also known as Woodstock Palace; until Tudor times it was an important stage on the monarchs' progresses around the country.
3   *VCH Oxon,* xii, 333.
4   *VCH Oxon,* xii, 369.
5   WBM B 82.
6   Six in 1580 Constitution, dropping to five in 1583 by further orders.
7   Guidebook to St. Mary Magdalene Church.
8   Ballard, Ch.iv, *Troublous times.*
9   Walter, *The Oxfordshire Rising,* Past & Present.
10   Spufford, 144.
11   See Fletcher family.
12   WBM B 78/2.
13   Chambers, 84.
14   Eddershaw, *Oxfordshire area in the civil war.*
15   WBM B 82.
16   WBM B 78/2, B 78/3, *WCBk.*
17   *WCA,* Vol. 58. ORO Churchwardens accounts.
18   ORO MSS. Wills (Oxon); PRO PROB 11.
19   See Appendix.
20   See 'Combined Families' chart.

Margaret Ayres' family tree

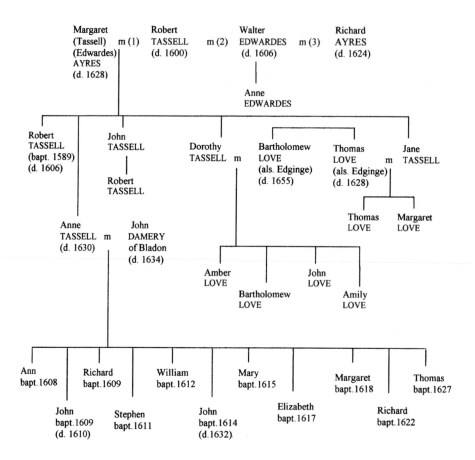

The story of Margaret Ayres, a widow of Hensington

Margaret was born before 1570 and married around 1585 but her birth surname has not been traced. Her first husband was Robert Tassell, described as a yeoman in his will of 1600.[1] Margaret and Robert had five children, Robert, John, Anne, Dorothy and Jane. Robert, the eldest son, was baptised at Bladon in 1589.

The family lived in Hensington in a 3-roomed house, part of the smallholding that provided their income. They grew wheat and barley on around 20 acres and kept livestock. An inventory of Robert's goods included poultry, cattle and over 50 sheep and lambs. The late 1590s were noted for several years of poor harvests and higher than usual mortality. Raising and feeding five children at that time must have caused the Tassell family some hardship and the loss of the breadwinner in 1600 would have been a further blow. Robert left cash for each of his children and the residue of his estate for Margaret's own use. Although she may have been well used to helping her husband with the livestock and marketing, managing a farm was heavy work for a woman and Margaret's five children, all below teenage, could not have provided her with sufficient labour to carry on alone. Margaret had little choice but to remarry in order to provide economic and practical support for her family. Robert Tassell's estate, valued at £48, provided her with an attractive 'dowry' to bring to a second marriage.

Margaret's next marriage, not documented, was of short duration. Her second husband was Walter Edwardes who died in 1606.[2] Described as a husbandman in his will, Walter's inventory shows the family lived in the same little house in Hensington that Margaret inherited from Robert Tassell. His base born daughter,[3] Anne Edwardes, was bequeathed £20 and there were cash legacies of £10 and £1 for Walter's brothers William, of Woodstock, and George, a cutler in London. Margaret's children were each left £5. All five were mentioned in Walter's will but the eldest son, Robert, missing from the administration documents, may have died at the same time as his stepfather.[4] Margaret was left £40 and residue of the estate, the smallholding that she brought to the marriage. Problems arose immediately after Walter's death; there was insufficient money to meet his legacies. The will's overseers, alderman Thomas Browne and John Dubber, were called in to verify and approve Margaret's computation whereby she arranged for all legatees to accept a proportion less than their original bequests from Walter. His daughter Anne agreed to accept £15, his brother William, £7.10s and the Tassell children £3 each. Two of Walter's legacies were cancelled; £1 for George Edwardes and a cupboard for widow Annis Castell of Hensington. Annis Castell may have been Anne Edwardes' mother; she named a married daughter, Anne Plant, in her will of 1626.[5] Some indication of Margaret's strong character emerged at this stage; she refused to sign the administration papers until George Edwardes' £1 legacy was crossed out. No reason was given; was it impractical to deliver such a small sum as far as London? Noticeably Margaret's legacy of £40 was not reduced.

There were no further family probates for nearly two decades, but inevitably many changes took place during that time. The children, all single at the time of their stepfather's death in 1606, were soon married. The only registered marriage, of Anne Tassell to John Damery of Bladon, took place there on 5th August 1607. Bladon registers list the baptisms of John and Anne's eleven children, born between 1608 and 1627, a large family for that time. Infant and childhood deaths were common but only two of the Damery family did not outlive their parents. However Anne Damery died in 1630 when she was in her late thirties; having come safely through her many pregnancies she was perhaps worn out by childbearing. Widower John Damery died in 1634. By that date most of their children were over eight years old and could legally be employed as servants or helped into apprenticeships by the parish overseers.[6] At the age of seven a child could legally choose his or her own guardian and the younger Damerys may have been fostered by their aunts or uncles.[7]

Margaret's daughters Jane and Dorothy Tassell made advantageous marriages to two brothers, Thomas and Bartholomew Love,[8] both Woodstock residents. Bartholomew, a glover, was implicated in a court action in 1609 for purchasing stolen sheepskins; however he was not penalised for receiving.[9] He was admitted freeman in 1635,[10] held office as churchwarden in 1636 and later became a member of the common council. In 1639 he was appointed chamberlain holding the post until 1646 when he was chosen alderman. He became mayor in the same year following the death of alderman Bennet Painter.[11] There are no probate documents for Bartholomew Love whose burial was registered at Woodstock on 12th March 1655.

Thomas Love, a woolman, died in June 1628, less than a month after his mother in law, Margaret Ayres. His death must have been unexpected as he was appointed executor of Margaret's will dated 7th May and both their wills were proved on 14th June 1628.[12] Thomas and Jane had a son and daughter, Thomas and Margaret; each was left

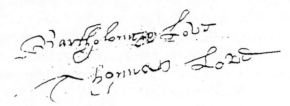

Signatures of Bartholomew and Thomas Love, brothers who married sisters Dorothy and Jane Tassell.

£10 to be paid on their marriage days. The Loves lived in a comfortable house and Thomas's goods were valued at £109. Jane Love, a comparatively wealthy widow in her thirties, probably remarried but no record has been traced. Her son, Thomas Love, continued to live in Woodstock and his family is traceable in the parish registers after 1654.

Woodstock documents of the time provide some information on Margaret's second son, John Tassell; he was licensed as a victualler in April 1618 and elected tithingman on the same day.[13] Admitted a freeman of Woodstock from 1621, he featured occasionally in the chamberlains' accounts but his name does not recur after 1630.

In October 1624 Richard Ayres of Hensington died intestate. The appraisers of his inventory included John Tassell and Bartholomew Love.[14] He lived in a small house with hall and chamber over and one lower chamber; his administratrix was his wife, Margaret Ayres. Richard was Margaret's third husband. His inventory shows that their small farm was still in production with crops on the fields and livestock in the yards; total value was £51, a similar sum to the two previous husbands' inventories. So the farm still flourished despite the couple's advancing years.

Signature of John Tassell; a brave attempt at the Christian name - the surname appears written by a different hand.

Margaret Ayres' third widowhood lasted until her death in 1628 when she was aged about 60. Her will, dated 7th May, lists some of her children and grandchildren.[15] Dorothy Love, wife of Bartholomew, is not mentioned and had perhaps died but her four children are named; sons Amber, Bartholomew and John and daughter Amily. Margaret favoured her son-in-law, Thomas Love, making him joint executor with her own son John Tassell. There was a legacy of a ewe and lamb for each of her grandsons who included Robert, son of John Tassell.

In Margaret's family none made a great contribution to the history of the borough and so are not well represented in writings of the time. However, the cluster of probate documents, outlining her life of hard work and many setbacks, provide an insight into life outside the main activities detailed in the town records. Many at that time would have led similar lives and Margaret's story illustrates well the use of wills and inventories for family reconstitution.

References

1   ORO MSS. Wills (Oxon), 65/2/26.
2   ORO MSS. Wills (Oxon), 20/1/51.
3   Base born = illegitimate.
4   Margaret's reference to 'my son Robert' in her will almost certainly means grandson.
5   ORO MSS. Wills (Oxon), 120/1/45.
6   Houlbrooke, 154.
7   Cox, 17, 21.
8   Love (als. Edginge).
9   WBM B78/2 f70v.
10   WCA, 157.
11   WCA, 234.
12   ORO MSS. Wills (Oxon), 139/1/31; 1/5/33.
13   WBM B78/3 – licenses issued at view of frankpledge.
14   ORO MSS. Wills (Oxon), 106:125; 295/1/29.
15   ORO MSS. Wills (Oxon), 1/5/33.

Family of Ralph Bradshaw with related families

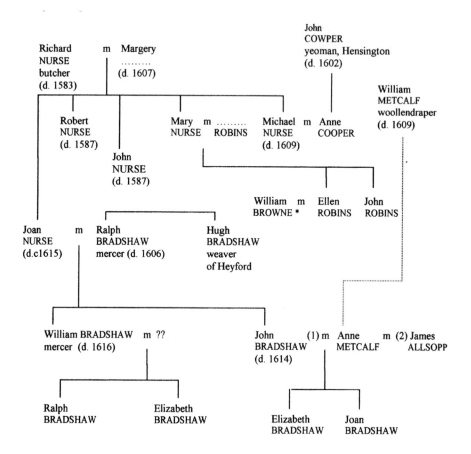

* see also Browne family tree

The family of Ralph Bradshaw

It is necessary to deal with the Bradshaws as two families. Ralph Bradshaw (d.1606) and Thomas Bradshaw (d.1613) flourished in the same period but research has provided no link between them or their respective families.

Ralph Bradshaw, a wealthy and successful mercer, apparently had a monopoly of that trade in late 16th century Woodstock. He is named as common councillor in town documents as early as the 1580 constitution.[1] Serving five years as chamberlain, from 1592 until 1597, he never became an alderman of the town.[2] From 1589 he was a suitor in the portmoot court appearing as pledge, witness or juror as required.[3]

Before 1583 Ralph married Joan, daughter of Richard Nurse, a Woodstock butcher, who died in that year.[4] Margery Nurse, Joan's mother, was related to John Ryley, a chandler who owned the premises, now Bartholomew House in Market Street, which later became one of the Bradshaw properties.[5] John Ryley died in 1589 (his is the earliest surviving inventory in Woodstock probate documents).[6] His workshop contained a furnace, tallow tubs and trough, tallow knives and candle moulds. John Bradshaw's 1613 inventory on the same site does not list candle-making equipment; however, that of Thomas Sparrow, (d.1678)[7] includes a workshop with furnace, tallow knives and moulds suggesting that the premises were a chief source of candles for the town for at least a century.

By 1598 Ralph Bradshaw was paying £5 yearly rent for the newly appointed woolbeam allowing him profits from statutory weighing of wool for local and visiting merchants and market traders.[8] He was also paying 1½d for his dwellinghouse and 2s for 10ft of street space outside his shop where he would have displayed his mercery wares for sale.[9] By 1601 he had built a shop on the site, identified as the north west corner of premises now the Feathers Hotel in Market Street.[10]

In the 1580's and 90's Ralph and Joan Bradshaw were much concerned with family matters. Following the death of Joan's father in 1583, two of her brothers, young bachelors Robert and John Nurse, both died in 1587.[11] Joan's mother, Margery, did not remarry although left a widow with five

Bartholomew House, 7 & 9 Market Street, site of mercers' premises throughout the 16th and 17th centuries. The name derives from the Bartholomew family, relatives of Elizabeth Sparrow (d.1693).

children, four of them unmarried. She must have relied upon her daughter and son in law for support in bringing up her remaining children; for instance Ralph Bradshaw was granted probate of the wills of Joan's two brothers, thus taking on the family's legal affairs. He was obviously an able businessman and well trusted by Woodstock folk of the time; several asked him to be overseer to their wills.

Ralph and Joan Bradshaw raised only two children. The elder son, William, was born before 1583 and John, the younger, before 1587; both appear unmarried at the time of their father's death in 1606. With no surviving will for Ralph Bradshaw, it is impossible to judge how his wealth was distributed within the family. Joan was granted administration of his estate, valued at £411, a high total in those days.[12]

In the early 17th century the present day Market Street in Woodstock was divided into separate areas with names such as Hogmarket, Beefmarket ('Beafmarket') and Beastmarket, reflecting its different trades and marketing sites. William Bradshaw was to inherit his grandmother's house in Hogmarket Street upon her death.[13] However she lived into old age and was still alive in 1606 when Ralph Bradshaw died, so William took over his late father's mercery premises; the rent rolls from 1609 to 1613 record him as owner/occupier of a dwellinghouse in Beefmarket Street at 1½d rent. In the same timespan he was also owner/occupier of a new shop and cellar in Beastmarket street, rebuilding the cellar by 1614.[14]

William was active in town affairs being listed as freeman and councillor in 1608.[15] He is regularly mentioned in the chamberlains' accounts and became chamberlain himself from 1612 to 1614 but, like his father, did not achieve the office of alderman.[16]

In 1608, a time of grain dearth, a census was called to evaluate stocks of grain held by the wealthier Woodstock residents.[17] William Bradshaw reported six persons in his household and having purchased 3 quarters of barley with an option on barley in the field worth £5.10s. William was probably married by this date and the six persons would have included his wife, his widowed mother, servants and possibly a young child. However, in his will of 1616 he mentioned only two children, both of minor age and needing guardians.[18] There may have been other children who did not survive. William's mother, Joan Bradshaw, died only shortly before him in 1616; Ralph Bradshaw's brother, Hugh, dealt with the administration of their estates and burials.

From 1611 some of William's servants and their friends were involved in ongoing thieving from his shop; there are lengthy accounts of criminal proceedings against them in the portmoot court book.[19] One ploy was to take items from the shop board (counter) having distracted Mrs. Bradshaw's attention while she was in charge of the shop. Long lists of stolen mercery wares and their values appear in these court examinations, providing details of the range of goods sold. In

Signature of Ralph Bradshaw, mercer (d. 1606).

1611 Walter Hollis, Bradshaw's servant, confessed to stealing lengths of flaxen cloth to make shirts for himself, and taking a blue leather purse for his girlfriend, Anne Cooper.[20] In 1612 John Barnes, a Woodstock tailor, admitted taking many yards of silk ribboning of yellow, white, black, blue and green with red ribbons always referred to as 'carnation'. On other occasions Barnes took silk buttons, skeins of coloured silk threads and lace trimmings. Later he progressed to taking lengths of holland, lockram[21] and canvas, from which his mother made him a doublet. Later Hollis admitted stealing women's stockings and silk garters for his girlfriend. At the end of these criminal proceedings some dozen or more Woodstock folk had been implicated as receivers of stolen goods. Some wrongdoers were sent to Oxford gaol and others punished at the local stocks and whipping post. Apart from the offer of a sow from Richard Barnes, husband of Anne, one of the receivers, there is no record of any recompense made to Bradshaw who must have suffered financially from this repetitive stealing.

William Bradshaw died in 1616 in early middle age. His will mentions two children, Ralph and Elizabeth, but not his wife who must have predeceased him. Elizabeth was left the substantial sum of £100 payable at age 18 or marriage, reverting to Ralph if she die earlier. Ralph was left the residue of the estate, including the mercery business and all property. William's uncle, Hugh Bradshaw, a weaver of Heyford Warren, and his friend William Metcalf, a Woodstock woollendraper,[22] were appointed executors and entrusted with management of profits from land holdings, together with tuition and guardianship of the two children until they inherit.[23] Perhaps Hugh Bradshaw died soon after William because young Ralph Bradshaw, being attested over seven years of age, appeared at the portmoot court in August 1618 and chose Ralph Clement, a tanner of Bicester, to become his guardian.[24] His appearance represents the only recorded use of this legal right in Woodstock courts.

The inventory of William's goods, drawn on 5th June 1616, was divided between household and shop wares. There were nine rooms, including a gallery over a great chamber with general household furnishings and separate lists of linen, pewter and silver. Wearing apparel of William's mother, 'old widow Bradshaw', and of his wife was appraised. The wife's was itemised and included a hat lined with velvet, a close fitting cap of blackwork called a coif ('quaife'), and fringed scarf and gloves. The latter would not have been included if the wife was still living as clothing was her personal property and not subject to valuation. Woodstock town residents were not often listed with livestock on their premises, so it is unusual to find William with stables housing three horses with their gear in Oxford Street with racks, mangers and a dung heap in the back yard. Some of his land holdings were appraised – a six year lease of a little garden next to his house with some hemp growing there at 25s[25] and a little close of land in Hensington at £4. He had grass in Hensington field purchased from John Cooper and more in Kidlington mead. The mercery wares in his shop, not itemised but valued separately at £74, brought the total inventory to £215 with additional shop debts of £83 thought irrecoverable.

John Bradshaw, younger son of Ralph and Joan, also became a mercer with his shop premises at Bartholomew House (now 7 and 9 Market Street).[26] When she died in 1607 Margery Nurse, John's grandmother, left the property to his brother William; 1609 rent rolls list a tenement in Hogmarket Street owned by William and occupied by John Bradshaw with a chantry rent of 10s. By December 1613 John had become both owner and occupier.

Following others of his family, John Bradshaw took his part in town affairs; he was churchwarden by 1608 and in that office travelled to Witney for the Bishop's visitation on occasions.[27] He is listed as borough freeman and common councillor from 1608 and also held office as tithingman and constable.[28]

John's wife was named Anne; she may have been the daughter of William Metcalf, a wealthy Woodstock woollendraper who occupied the present day post office site. Metcalf died in 1609 leaving his married daughters, including Anne Bradshaw, just five pounds apiece, but there is indication he had already provided each of them with a generous marriage settlement of one hundred pounds, since he left that amount to an unmarried daughter 'as her porcion'.[29] The christian name of William Bradshaw's wife has not been discovered and without this information it is impossible to certify which of the Bradshaw brothers, William or John, married Anne Metcalf.

John and Anne Bradshaw had two daughters, Joan and Elizabeth. In his 1613 will John left them 100 marks each, reverting to William's son Ralph if neither survived. His dwellinghouse in Woolmarket Street was left to widow Anne for her life and then to the two girls. Anne was appointed executrix and two supervisors were charged with paying her £10 yearly from profits of investing the 100 marks.[30] The supervisors, Joan Bradshaw, John's widowed mother and Hugh Bradshaw, his uncle, both a generation older than John, may not have been the wisest choice. Strangely he thought Anne might renounce custody of the children and the supervisors were to default on her £10 annuity if this happened. One possible reason for a refusal of custody is that Anne was not the girls' mother. According to the Nurse family probate documents John was born between 1583 and 1587. He could have married twice, but died aged around thirty, so this seems unlikely.

John Bradshaw's inventory amounted to £178. His house contained hall, parlour and shop each with a chamber over; a lease was valued at £6. The most interesting part of the inventory is an itemised list of shop goods: 375 ells[31] of canvas valued at over £19, 25 ells of flaxen cloth at 33s with smaller quantities of cloth called buffins, tuftaffity, bastard millen, fustian, sackcloth, linen, lynsey wolsey, holland and lawn.[32] Trimmings included silken lace and ribbons, there were 54 dozen of silk buttons, 6 dozen of silver buttons, sewing silks and other threads, gartering and boothose. The shop also sold a range of grocery and household wares including sugar loaves, spices, starch, soap, salt, pitch and turpentine. Other varied goods were glasses, coney skins, gunpowder, aniseed, liquorice and hops; 'remnants of tobacco ('tabaco') and a pot' were valued at 5s.

Widow Anne Bradshaw re-married soon after John's death. In November 1615 with her second husband, James Allsopp, she pursued a debt on John's estate in the portmoot court.[33] The Allsopps do not appear in contemporary documents and may have moved away from Woodstock.

Of the Bradshaw children only Ralph is traceable; he returned to Woodstock in the 1630's. The chamberlains

A Corporation Seal of 1461.[35] Such seals were used to validate documents such as property conveyances.

reported 2s 1d owing for his rents in 1635; however he was disposing of his property by 1640 when Thomas Hawten used the town seal for his fine (conveyance) from Ralph Bradshaw. In 1641 Nicholas Mayott paid 4s for the seal in a similar transaction.[34]

On his death in 1647 Richard Reade, a Woodstock butcher, owed 40s to Ralph Bradshaw of London[36] and this apparently concludes the family's connection with Woodstock. No marriages have been traced for William's daughter, Elizabeth, or her cousins Joan and Elizabeth, daughters of John Bradshaw.

References

1   WBM B 82.
2   WBM B 81.
3   *WCBk.*
4   ORO MSS. Wills (Oxon), 47/1/3.
5   *VCH Oxon*, xii, 347.
6   ORO MSS. Wills (Oxon), 147/1/12.
7   ORO MSS. Wills (Oxon), 62/1/9.
8   The woolbeam was a device to check the weight of wool sold in the marketplace.
9   WBM Rent rolls *f87.*
10 *VCH Oxon,* xii, 359.
11 ORO MSS. Wills (Oxon), 47/1/12; 47/1/13.
12 ORO MSS. Wills (Oxon), 106:15.
13 ORO MSS. Wills (Oxon), 47/2/2.
14 *WCA*, 30.
15 WBM B78/2 *f44.*
16 *WCA*, 232.
17 WBM B78/2 *f59.*
18 ORO MSS. Wills (Oxon), 4/4/17.
19 WBM B78/2 from 1611.
20 See also Cooper family.
21 Holland – smooth hard wearing linen (OED); lockram – coarse linen (Collins).
22 Woollen-draper – dealer in woollen goods (Collins).
23 ORO MSS. Wills (Oxon), 4/4/17.
24 WBM B78/3 *f133v.*
25 Hemp used for weaving.
26 *VCH Oxon*, xii, 347.
27 *WCA*, 4.
28 WBM B78/2 *passim.*
29 PRO PROB. 11/111.20.
30 ORO MSS. Wills (Oxon), 4/3/45.
31 Ell – an old measure of length, about 45 inches (OED).
32 Tuftaffity – a rich taffeta with tufted pile (Collins); fustian – a thick twill cloth of short nap (OED); sackcloth – a coarse fabric of flax or hemp (OED); lynsey wolsey – a fabric of coarse wool woven on cotton warp (Collins); lawn – fine cotton or linen for wearing clothes (OED).
33 WBM B78/3 *f52.*
34 *WCA*, 183.
35 Ballard – title page.
36 ORO MSS. Wills (Oxon), 299/7/40.

Family of Thomas Bradshaw

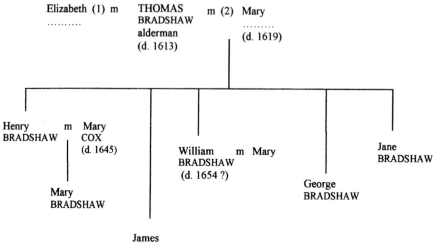

The family of Thomas Bradshaw

There is no indication that Thomas Bradshaw, innkeeper, was related to Ralph Bradshaw, mercer, though both flourished in the late 16th and early 17th centuries. If they were related (by dates of death Ralph and Thomas could have been brothers) it seems the two had no dealings with each other. Probate documents are the most likely to reveal links but neither family mentions the other.

The story of Thomas Bradshaw's family is largely that of Thomas himself. As innkeeper of the Bull, a leading 16th century inn, he became a successful and apparently self-important Woodstock resident in the late 16th and early 17th centuries.[1] The Bull was used as a headquarters by courtiers accompanying Princess Elizabeth at the time of her detention at the manor in Woodstock Park during the rule of her sister Mary Tudor. Sir Henry Bedingfield, her custodian, thought the Bull 'a marvellous colourable place'.[2]

Thomas Bradshaw was established as common councillor by 1580[3] and by then was described as a gentleman, implying that he lived on acquired wealth rather than manual labour. He was chosen chamberlain in 1595 sharing office with mercer Ralph Bradshaw; the only time the two surnames were associated in office. Thomas was always present at the chamberlains' annual audit until 1612.[4] Having served as chamberlain he was eligible for aldermanship on the death of John Williams in 1602. He served two terms as mayor, 1604 to 1606 and 1608 to 1610, but he would have exercised most power as Justice of the Peace, an office he held from before 1608 until his death in 1613.

From 1588 to 1595 Thomas appeared in the portmoot court record as plaintiff in two actions for debt and defendant in a further two; he also appeared as pledge or bailor for other suitors. With his wife, Elizabeth, he entered into a conveyance for Richard Wryte's house in 1591.[5]

By the next portmoot court record in 1607 Thomas Bradshaw JP was sitting regularly alongside fellow JP Thomas Browne at the twice-yearly sessions, hearing evidence for and against local and travelling felons. As mayor in November 1608 he was required by the laws of central government to appoint a jury and report numbers in households and stocks of grain held by wealthier townsfolk at a time of approaching dearth. However there was no report of Thomas's grain holdings or the number of persons in his house although other innkeepers were included and in total 29 households were assessed. When viewed alongside probate documents this survey provides a useful guide to family size in Woodstock.[6] Books of Dearth Orders, issued as necessary by central government for enforcement by local JPs, aimed to regulate the price and ration supplies of grain. Other years of dearth were 1586, the late 1590's and 1622.[7]

An entry in licensing sessions in April 1608 shows Thomas was sometimes at odds with other town officers; Edmund Hiorne, town clerk, wrote cynically 'Thomas Abbott was licensed by Mr mayor only and Mr Thomas Bradshewe did deign to give his consent thereunto'.[8] A further memo states 'Mr. Bradshewe did say in open court that he would keep piping and dauncing in his house at 10 and one o'clock in the night hereafter', implying Thomas felt himself above the rules for lesser townsmen. At another session in October 1610 he denied a victualling licence to John Taylor even though the mayor and Thomas Browne were willing to allow one.[9]

Both chamberlains' accounts and portmoot court record include accounts of Thomas Bradshaw taking charge of horses when strays or forfeits for unlawful dealing. Stabling was one of the main services offered at the Bull; noblemen and gentry visiting Woodstock and the king's manor house would have stayed at the inn (premises now National Westminster Bank) where there was ample stabling in the long rear yard.

A list of debtors and creditors appended to Thomas's will in 1613 proved he was well acquainted with local gentry, enjoying their company and lifestyle. Locally he owed £30 to Jerome Kyte, lawyer and maltster who became JP on Thomas' death, and £10 to Mistress Leake, widow of Robert, a gentlewoman of a wealthy family. The list of Thomas's debtors was even more impressive including several knights; Sir Henry Stoner owed £5, Sir Henry Lee £14 and Sir Henry Lee, baronet, a debt for Sir Henry Lee, knight of the garter.[10] The latter Sir Henry, who died in 1611, had been Champion for Queen Elizabeth and lived nearby at Ditchley. As high steward of the borough, he often received gifts of sugar loaves and cakes from Woodstock and would have dined at the Bull.

Appraisers of Thomas Bradshaw's inventory were Humphrey Fitzharbert esquire of Begbroke, an honorary freeman of the town,[11] Jerome Nash esquire of Old Woodstock, one of the area's wealthiest gentry,[12] Jerome Kyte, a creditor, mentioned above and William Metcalf, local woollen draper. The inventory value was £242 and listed many luxuries beginning with wearing apparel, some items of note are satin doublets of black and yellow, silk stockings and garters, nightcaps of satin, velvet and worsted and three each of cloaks, gowns and shirts. He could have carried a rapier with choice of four daggers and owned a looking glass in order to see what a fine figure he presented. Hoods and bells for hawks and a drawing box indicate leisure pursuits. Thomas had received a good education; his books included Holinshed's Chronicle and there was a Bible in folio and the Book of Common Prayer.

The inventory identifies the guest – rooms at the Bull, each given a name or symbol – a great chamber, cofferers' chamber, star and falconers ('fawkners') chambers. The half

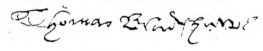

Signature of Alderman Thomas Bradshaw.

moon and cross dagger chambers were sparsely furnished and not for the more important guests. A chamber was reserved for Mary Bradshaw, Thomas's widow, and a maid's chamber for her servant.[13]

Large quantities of linen, as would be expected for a prominent inn, included forty pairs of sheets and 14 dozen napkins. Plenty of utensils for preparation and cooking of food were listed but tableware of plate, pewter, brass etc., was not itemised being valued at £25, £10 and £13 respectively. For such a flamboyant character Thomas's will was comparatively simple; he directed all his goods to be sold to pay his debts and the remaining money divided between his family. Mary, described as his 'welbeloved wife', received £40, son George £30 and son William an unreadable sum. Only daughter, Jane, received £66; the residue was divided between eldest sons, Henry and James, as executors. Henry's daughter Mary, apparently the only grandchild at that time, was left £2.13s 4d for payment on her marriage day or age eighteen.

Thomas possibly married twice; in a conveyance of March 1591 his wife is named Elizabeth, but in 1613 he was married to Mary.[14] Both Thomas and Mary mention five children and one grandchild in their wills, indicating that Elizabeth must have died in the early 1590's.

Thomas Bradshaw's death is well documented and involves a supposed case of witchcraft.[15] In May 1613 widow Joyce Coles appeared before the mayor and JPs on suspicion of felony of witchcraft. Reportedly Jane Bradshaw, daughter of Thomas, had said to her 'good day goodwife[16] Coles' and Coles replied 'why do you say to me "good day goodwife Coles" for your father cannot abide me? But it is no matter, he will prosper never the better for it'. Jane Bradshaw attested that soon afterwards her

Signature of Jane Bradshaw, daughter of Thomas; she has spelled her surname 'Brashore'.

father fell sick and at the time of the hearing 'lay lame on his limbs' and could not turn himself in bed without great help. Witchcraft could be a capital offence but the courts were careful in judgments of these cases. The chamberlains' accounts show that Joyce was confined to prison for a time but in December 1613 the town expenses included 'a shroud for the widow Coles' who clearly did not survive long after her ordeal.[17]

Thomas Bradshaw died on 2nd June 1613. His symptoms as described by his daughter suggest he had suffered a stroke. His character could be described 'larger than life' and thus his presence would have been missed by Woodstock folk even those who had suffered his overbearing conduct in town affairs.

Thomas left four sons and one daughter but none attained the high offices held by their father. Henry Bradshaw, eldest son, described as 'gent', became innholder at the Bull until 1615 when alderman Joseph Harris, successor to Thomas Bradshaw took over.[18]

Henry Bradshaw held junior offices becoming councillor and constable in 1619 and appeared on inhabitants' lists until 1626 when present at a muster.[19] Henry's wife and daughter Mary are mentioned in his mother's will of 1619. Henry's brothers, George and James, feature little in Woodstock documents of the time; James may have died soon after Thomas as he is missing from the will's probate clause although named joint executor with Henry.[20]

William Bradshaw, son of Thomas (not to be confused with William, son of Ralph) is mentioned in chamberlains' accounts until 1631 when he owed the town 3s 4d to supply a bucket, a requirement on obtaining freedom.[21] Buckets were kept in the guildhall in readiness if fire occurred in town.

In 1645 widow Mary Bradshaw, apparently resident in London made her will describing herself as 'late of Woodstock'.[22] She was probably the widow of Henry Bradshaw, son of Thomas; she mentioned her brother, William Bradshaw, who was left £20 and a suit of her husband's clothes, and 'cousins' Jane and Mary Bradshaw as well as John Cox her 'owne brother'. Jane may have been the daughter of Thomas (d. 1613). There were legacies of up to £10 for family members and friends but Mary mentioned no children of her own. The will suggests a somewhat disrupted life. Having lived in Cassington before removing to London, she had household goods and 'writings'[23] left with goodwife Warner of Longcombe.[24] However, the most intriguing legacy is to the executrix, Jane Bradshaw, to be handed over by goodwife Warner and described as 'the tenn poundes which shee and I hidd in the house att Cassenton'. In view of the date this might have been intended as a safeguard against any future losses occasioned by the civil war.

Mary Bradshaw's will brings to an end the family association with the town. When parish registers begin only one burial, that of William Bradshaw in March 1655, may relate to the family.

References

1   *VCH Oxon*, xii, 338.
2   Plowden, Alison, *The Young Elizabeth*, 180, (Sutton Publishing), 1971.
3   WBM B 82.
4   WBM B 81.
5   *WCBk*, 34.
6   WBM B78/2 *f58v*.
7   Slack, 3.
8   WBM B78/2 *f18*.
9   WBM B78/2 *f131v*.
10   ORO MSS. Wills (Oxon), 4/3/17.
11   WBM B78/3 *f259*.
12   See Nash family.
13   ORO MSS. Wills (Oxon), 4/3/17.
14   *WCBk*, 34.
15   WBM B78/2 *f262v*.
16   Goodwife – female head of household (OED).
17   *WCA*, 126.
18   *WCA*, 60.
19   WBM B96 *f33v*. Musters were meetings called to assess the numbers of men available to fight for the king if war threatened. Towns were required also to list any weapons and armour.
20   ORO MSS. Wills (Oxon), 4/6/12.
21   *WCA*, 138.
22   PRO PROB 11/194.175.
23   probably legal documents.
24   Longcombe = Combe, Oxon.

Browne and associated families

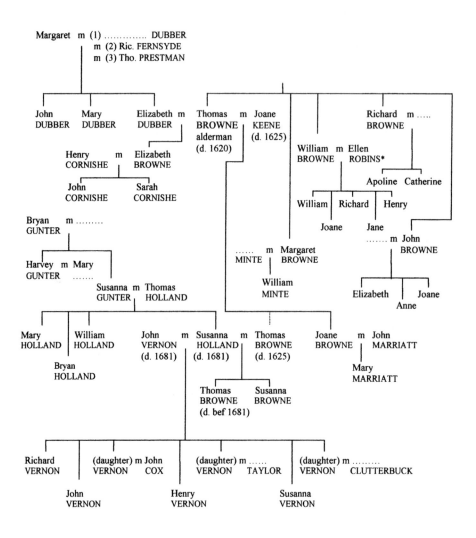

*see also family of Ralph Bradshaw

Thomas Browne and family of Woodstock

The story of the Browne family's association with Woodstock can be told within the lifetime of one member, Thomas Browne. He was a native of Chipping Norton; the surname occurs in that town's parish registers but his baptism is not recorded. He arrived in Woodstock as a young man in the late 1560's. Thomas attended Oxford church courts in 1593 regarding a local will and attested to have been resident in Woodstock for 27 years.[1]

By 1580 he was well settled into the borough as a common councillor.[2] The same year he was signatory to an order disfranchising alderman George Whitton, comptroller of Woodstock park, following a quarrel with the then mayor, William Skelton.[3] In 1588 Thomas became an alderman, a position held for life. He served several terms as mayor, the earliest in 1591; he was a JP from 1608 until his death in 1620. These combined offices made Thomas Browne an influential resident for four decades.

Browne was a maltster, an occupation often associated with wealthier residents; as a borough freeman he made full use of the portmoot court to settle debts and other business matters. The court book from 1588 to 1595 records 12 actions of debt and trespass brought by him, mainly against Woodstock men, some for amounts of several pounds. The court book of 1608 to 1614 records 15 more actions for debt and that from 1614 to 1622, a further 8.[4] Throughout these years he was one of the most frequent users of the court.

In addition to his appearances as suitor Thomas was kept very busy with other court duties, presiding at every hearing during his terms as mayor and sitting as JP at the twice-yearly court leet or view of frankpledge. Also during his mayoral years he would have officiated as clerk of the market and overseen assizes of bread and ale etc. His magistrate's duties included presiding at frequent hearings or 'examinations' of miscreants brought before the court for offences such as petty thieving and disorderly behaviour. Sometimes magistrates heard more serious crimes such as horse stealing and bodily assault; these were usually referred to

Oxford courts.[5] As an alderman Browne attended the majority of council meetings and yearly audits of chamberlains' and churchwardens' accounts. His final appearance as JP was in June 1620 when he heard three actions brought for breach of the peace and one for child maintenance.[6]

Portmoot court books also contain details of property transactions, conveyances etc., and Thomas Browne was sometimes involved as signatory to these dealings. In 1593 he may have been acting as family adviser to Margaret Prestman when witnessing the conveyance of William Rathbone's house to her grandson Richard Dubber in accordance with her late husband's will.[7] On two occasions Thomas was party to conveyances of property proclaimed in court. The first, in 1613, recorded his purchase of two properties from the Collingwood family and a second, in 1616, his sale of a close of pasture and granary to John and Hester Whitton.[8]

The Woodstock rent rolls outline Thomas Browne's steady acquisition of property.[9] In 1598 he was paying £4 annual rent for land in the corporation meadows known as the common or ley pool, 6s8d for his dwellinghouse at the park gate and 6d quit rent for another house. In 1608/9 he was still paying 6s8d rent for the park gate property.

A corporation lease of 1607[10] mentions a garden and tenement belonging to Thomas Brown 'sometime Fletchers land' identified as part of the site which Thomas referred to by that name in his 1620 will. This property had belonged to the influential Fletcher family for most of the 16th century; the last owner being Henry Fletcher, ironmonger, who died in 1595;[11] Henry's widow, Margery, later

Signature of Alderman Thomas Browne (d. 1620).

became Browne's tenant. Maybe she felt unfairly treated by this arrangement, because in 1617 she entered a claim in the portmoot court for three parts of the seven messuages owned by Browne. However, Edmund Hiorne, clerk of court, wrote 'Mr. Browne's records are all written in paper remaining with my precedents ('presidents'), and Mr. Browne hath it in parchment under Mr.Mayor's seal'. Her claim was dismissed.[12]

Additionally, by 1608/9 Browne had built a malthouse next to the river described as 'neer unto the bayes' which attracted a rent of £5 per annum.[13] Further entries in that year's rent rolls list 6d for Browne's tenement where Margery Fletcher dwelt, described as 'in Oxon' Street near the

Fletchers House. The view from the garden shows the gables of the 'great house' built by Thomas Browne c. 1614.

corn market hill' (the present day Market Place is identified as Cornmarket Hill)[14] also a rent of 1½d for a tenement of John Rokesby in Oxford Street 'near Robin Hood's elm' and 4d for a house where Mr.Hitch dwelt in Beastmarket 'with 2d for his oven'.

By 1614 Browne was paying rent for the ley pool, his house at park gate, his riverside malthouse and houses of Margery Fletcher, John Oakley (formerly Rokesby) and Mr. Hitch. In addition, in February of that year, he acquired from the Collingwood family houses known as Maynards and Mundayes Place with a combined rent of 4s10d.[15] Adjoining his previous purchase of the Fletcher's site the latter gave him probably the most prestigious address in town. Opposite the church and near the market place and guildhall, the former Collingwood houses adjoined Fletchers' property and Browne's property thereby covered some 5 burgage plots extending to Frog Lane (now Harrisons) on its north side and Blackhall Lane (now Browns Lane) on its east. On the Collingwood site he built himself a great house which he called 'Fletchers'.[16] This house is described in detail in the inventory of Joane Browne, his widow, who died in 1625.[17] Thomas Browne's own will of 1620 shows that he converted the Fletchers' slaughterhouse into a malthouse; the grounds included gardens and an orchard.[18]

In addition to his many civic activities, the Church may have been one of Thomas Browne's chief interests. The chamberlains' accounts show the Brownes among families regularly claiming expenses for entertaining visiting preachers; in 1615 for instance they were allowed 2s for wine and sugar for a preacher at Christmas and 4s4d for others throughout the year.[19] In 1620, with his son about to be installed as Rector of Bladon with Woodstock parish, Thomas bequeathed £10 to the town to provide two sermons preached annually at Christmas and Easter. He also remembered his birthplace, Chipping Norton, with a similar bequest of £5 for an annual New Year's Day sermon.

The wills of the two Thomas Brownes, father and son, were both proved in the Prerogative Court of Canterbury, indicating ownership of property in more than one diocese. Thomas senior left money to the poor of Wootton under Edge in Gloucestershire. In Woodstock he left his 'house called Fletchers' to his wife, Joane, for life and on her death to Thomas junior reverting to daughter Elizabeth Cornishe if Thomas died childless and similarly to youngest daughter Joane Marriatt. Joane Browne also received a half share of 'the ley pool',[20] his malthouse lease, and £200 the year after his death.

Thomas Browne senior married twice. The phrase 'my now wife' in his will indicates this.[21] His first wife may have been Elizabeth Dubber, whose mother, Margaret, married three times; firstly Elizabeth's father, then Richard Fernsyde and finally Thomas Prestman. When Richard Fernsyde died in 1570 he left Margaret with three children, named John, Mary and Elizabeth Dubber, all aged under 21.[22] As a second-time widow Margaret Fernsyde later married Thomas Prestman, a Woodstock shoemaker and common councillor until his death in 1590.[23] Prestman's will names three sons-in-law, John Dubber, Nicholas Stratton and Thomas Browne. At that time the term 'son-in-law' could mean a stepson as well as a daughter's husband, so possibly Prestman was referring to his stepson John Dubber and to his two stepdaughters' husbands, Nicholas Stratton and Thomas Browne. This was further borne out when Thomas Browne, as overseer, probated Thomas Prestman's will on 31st May 1590 for executrix Margaret Prestman. The Browne family traditionally named the eldest son and daughter after the parents; because Thomas Browne's eldest daughter was named Elizabeth this suggests that Thomas's first wife was Elizabeth, rather than Mary, Dubber.

Thomas Browne junior was born about 1596.[24] It is difficult to judge if he was the son of Elizabeth (nee Dubber) or Joane (nee Keene) who became Thomas's second wife. Thomas's second marriage is not recorded but must have taken place before the turn of the 16th/17th century because a second daughter, named Joane after her mother, was of age and already married when Thomas senior died in 1620.

Joane Keene also had family connections with Chipping Norton and these continued when Thomas's elder daughter Elizabeth married Henry Cornishe of that town. Thomas's will named their two children, John and Sarah. Henry Cornishe was a wealthy mercer and from 1616 held a lease of the local mill situated in Old Woodstock.[25] There was a dispute in 1628 over responsibility for repairing the mill bridge; the town took an indictment requiring Cornishe to effect repairs but he claimed responsibility lay with the King as lessor.[26] Henry Cornishe became a leading resident of Chipping Norton, founding almshouses there; his name lives on in Cornish Road. After the restoration, perhaps because of his puritan sympathies, he was taken and imprisoned at Oxford castle whereupon his nephew, William Diston of Chipping Norton, was forced to borrow £600 for his ransom.[27]

Thomas Browne junior may have attended the newly established Grammar School in Woodstock. He is probably the same Thomas Browne, gent, who studied at Exeter College, Oxford, matriculated in May 1612 aged 16 and gained a BA in 1615 and MA in 1618.[28] By will he left money to buy a book for Exeter College.[29] Thomas took Holy Orders and was appointed Rector of Bladon and Woodstock in 1621 under the patronage of John Whitton, gent, by grant from Charles, Prince of Wales.[30]

Thomas Browne junior married Susanna, youngest daughter of Thomas Holland, Regius Professor of Theology in Oxford University.[31] This young couple (Susanna was born in 1601) were soon to be parted, Thomas died in 1625, in his mid-twenties. They had a son, Thomas, born before his grandfather's death in 1620 and a daughter, Susanna, baptised at Bladon on 27th August 1623;[32] both children named after their parents in family tradition.

Soon after the untimely death of her husband in 1625 young widow Susanna Browne married John Vernon, also a Clerk in Holy Orders.[33] The Vernons took the living of Hanbury in Worcestershire where they remained until their deaths, both in 1681. John's will reveals they had many more children and that Susanna's son Thomas Browne died before his mother, leaving one daughter surviving him.[34] A memorial inscription

Signature of Thomas Browne, clerk, (d.1625). As Rector of Woodstock he signed himself 'parson'.

in Hanbury church tells the Vernon's story; there were eleven children, only five surviving their parents. Two of these, John and Susan set up the memorial to their parents 'in token of their deep respect ...sorrow and grief'. Susanna Vernon is described 'a pious, pleasant and modest wife'.

Joane, younger daughter of Thomas Browne senior, was almost certainly the daughter of Joane (nee Keene). Married to John Marriatt, she was favoured over her brother and sister in the will of widow Joane Browne in 1625.[35] Also she took over administration of her mother's estate from Susanna Browne, widow and executor of Thomas junior who had died just two weeks after his mother.

There is much information for family historians in the Browne wills. Thomas senior names his four brothers and one sister, with small legacies for each of them and for each of their children, who are also individually named.[36] There are bequests of money to buy rings for family and friends and forty shillings for John Dubber described as his brother in law and appointed overseer. Although Thomas's brothers can be identified as residents of Woodstock they did not follow him into town goverment, perhaps preferring to attend to their own trades. Thomas's will, dated 9th November 1620, was proved by his executor, Thomas junior, on 23rd January 1621/2.[37]

The will of Thomas junior, dated 23rd February 1625, also provides family information though mainly on his in-laws. He names his wife's mother, uncle and grandfather leaving them all small bequests for rings. The bulk of his wealth went to his son and daughter with legacies of £100 each. As was the custom he requested his friend Sir Jarrett Fleetwood, described as 'Knight of the Manor of Woodstock', to invest the legacies for their benefit until aged 21 and 18 respectively. There was a family dispute with Thomas's sister and brother in law, Joane and John Marriatt, who had made a claim on Thomas senior's estate; Thomas forgave them their debts to him and directed his executrix to deliver them their bonds. His will was proved by his widow, Susanna, on 9th March 1625.[38]

The final probate documents for the family are those of Joane Browne, widow of Thomas senior, proved in the Oxford courts on 4th August 1625.[39] Her will, dated 6th February 1625, contained many bequests of household goods to family and friends and she left her husband's horsemans coat to John Dubber whom she described as her brother in law. Granddaughter Mary Marriatt, daughter of John and Joane, was main beneficiary with a bequest of £100, this to be invested for her by William Metcalf and Edmund Hiorne, then mayor and town clerk of Woodstock. The £100 reverted to any other children of John and Joane Marriatt should Mary die before 21 or marriage, and in default to Thomas and Susanna Browne's children. Mary Marriatt also received some family silver, two salts, and 12 spoons, which Thomas Browne was to buy from her 'if he would have them'. Joane Marriatt was left £40 to be invested by William Metcalf and Edmund Hiorne for her maintenance while married to John Marriatt but to be paid to her upon his death or to their children if she predeceased him. It is unusual to find money being invested by trustees for the benefit of a married woman; this clearly suggests that Joane mistrusted John Marriatt. Elizabeth Cornishe, referred to as 'my daughter Cornishe, wife of Henry Cornishe of Chipping Norton' was left a silver spoon and her two children, at the end of the will as if an afterthought, a silver spoon apiece. Thomas Browne junior, referred to throughout as 'my son' was sole executor. There were debts due to Joane, mainly a few pounds or shillings, from well known Woodstock residents.

There is a suspicious, nuncupative, codicil to Joane's will, attested by William Metcalf, stating that Joane Browne later decided the forty pounds to be invested for Joane Marriatt should be used instead by John Marriatt to buy or lease some lifetime estate for his wife.

Joane Browne's inventory is dated 26th February 1625. Items listed room by room show the house comprised a hall, parlour, buttery, kitchen, a chamber over the parlour and another chamber referred to as 'William's chamber'; there may have been other rooms not included which did not contain any of Joane's possessions.[40] Her wearing apparel was valued at £10, and there was £21 ready money in the house. The most valuable item was malt, both ready-dried and green, together with some barley, appraised at 140 quarters value £126. The kitchen contained brewing equipment; there were hop poles and pigs in the yard and flitches of bacon indoors. Cloth and sewing yarns in the parlour indicated that Joane was a seamstress and in an upstairs chamber was a satin cushion, pawned to her, valued at £1 10s.

Accounts were produced by Joane Marriatt after she had legally taken over administration of her mother's estate from Susanna Browne. Interestingly, when the account was presented, after paying out legacies and writing off debts, Joane had disposed of all but £2 7s.9d of the total of £222 13s. Joane Browne had distrusted her son in law John Marriatt and perhaps his handiwork can be seen in the creative accountancy used in management of these legacies. He also took his time to hand over £10 bequest to the town from Mary Keene, Joane Browne's sister who died in 1626.[41] The Marriatts do not appear prominently in local documents but in the late 1640s were still mentioned in connection with the rent of Hitch's house, which had belonged to Thomas Browne senior early in the century.

Due to his involvment in Woodstock civic affairs Thomas Browne the elder is among the best documented townsmen of the 16th and 17th centuries. Records in Woodstock borough muniments provide a useful guide to his early life and detail many of his transactions and dealings with other townsfolk. Although Thomas Browne's brothers remained in Woodstock, the family's presence and influence in Woodstock must have been noticeably absent after the almost simultaneous deaths of Joane and Thomas Browne junior in 1625.

References

1   Howard-Drake, No. 35.
2   WBM B82.
3   See Whitton family.
4   WBM B 78/2, B 78/3, *WCBk*.
5   WBM B78/2 *passim*.
6   WBM B78/3 *202v, 203*.
7   *WCBk*, 68.
8   WBM B78/3 *ff3v, 65v*.
9   WBM B96.
10 WBM 64/1/1.
11 ORO MSS. Wills (Oxon), 187:344.
12 WBM B78/3 *f101v*.
13 WBM B96. The malthouse stood on present day White Hart site at corner of Brook Hill and Oxford Street.
14 *VCH Oxon*, xii, 336.
15 WBM B78/3 *65v*.
16 *VCH Oxon*, xii, 350.
17 ORO MSS. Wills (Oxon), 5/2/9.
18 PRO PROB. 11/137.
19 *WCA*, 61.
20 This part of the ley pool was known in the later 17th century as 'Browne's Mead'.
21 PRO PROB. 11/137.
22 ORO MSS. Wills (Oxon), 185:711.
23 ORO MSS. Wills (Oxon), 50/1/59.
24 *Alumni Oxoniensis 1500-1714* lists Browne aged 16 at matriculation in 1612.
25 *VCH Oxon*, xii, 429.
26 *WCA*, 122.
27 Eddershaw, 164.
28 *Alumni Oxoniensis 1500-1714*.
29 PRO PROB.11/145.

30 Guidebook to St.Mary Magdalene Church, Woodstock.
31 Memorial inscription in Hanbury Church, Worcs., (information supplied by Hereford and Worcester Record Office).
32 Bladon Parish Registers.
33 John Vernon, MA Balliol, May 1624. *Clerus.*
34 Hereford and Worcester Record Office – will of John Vernon, clerk, 13th August 1681 (no ref.).
35 ORO MSS. Wills (Oxon), 5/2/9.
36 See Browne family tree.
37 PRO PROB. 11/137.
38 PRO PROB. 11/145.
39 ORO MSS. Wills (Oxon), 5/2/9.
40 Grundon, 35.
41 *WCA, fn,* 111. ORO MSS. Wills (Oxon), 39/3/1.

Cooper family of Hensington

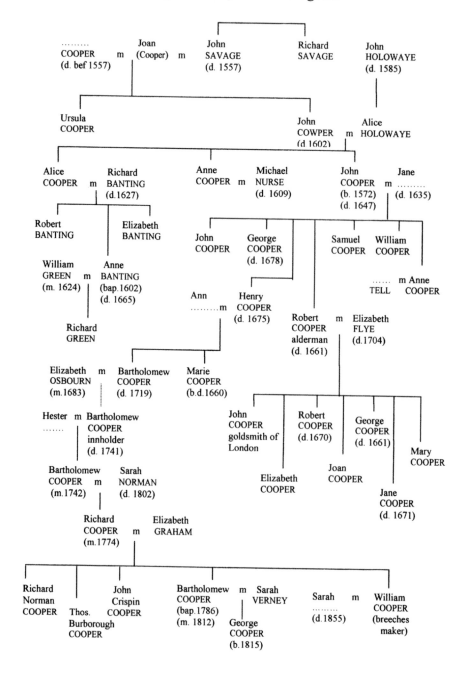

The Cooper family of Hensington

Woodstock was founded by Henry II in the mid-12th century. Created on about 60 acres outside the walls of a royal park containing the kings' manor house, the site was laid out in burgage plots enclosing a large triangular market place. The existing parishes of Wootton to the north of the river Glyme, Bladon on the south and Hensington on the east allowed no spread of boundaries in any direction, thus leaving no space for agricultural land for the town's use. Although some Woodstock residents retained plots in the common fields of Old Woodstock and Hampton meads, local yeomen and husbandmen lived and worked mainly in Hensington where land was available.

Hensington, part of Bladon parish and founded before the domesday census, functioned independently of Woodstock to some extent and could be called a close-knit community. Noticeably family surnames occur regularly in probate documents with neighbours, friends and relatives acting as witnesses, legatees, appraisers and overseers. It is through these Hensington probate documents that the early Cooper family can be traced. They became one of the foremost families, related to Bantings and Holloways. Other surnames found in Hensington documents are Abbott, Bruce, Harris, Slatter and Symonds.

An early reference to the Cooper family occurs in 1557. The will of John Savage of Hensington contains the bequest 'to twayne of my wyffe's children, that is to say John Cooper and Ursula Cooper as it doth appear by the testament of their late father – £4'.[1] Thus John and Ursula were the children of their mother's first marriage and the Cooper family probably establised in Hensington before the middle of the 16th century.

In his 1585 will John Holowaye, a Hensington labourer, names his daughter, Alice, married to John Cooper and their son John Cooper the younger. Anne Cooper also mentioned must be John and Alice's daughter. In contrast to John Savage, Holowaye was not wealthy. Whereas Savage left acres of barley and wheat to his family and bushels of barley to neighbours, John Holowaye's legacies, except the lease of his house, were of a few shillings or pence only.[2]

The elder John Cooper (usually spelled Cowper) concentrated on raising his family and making a living from agriculture; he may have inherited some of John Savage's land through his mother although most had been divided between Savage's own children on his death. In 1594 Thomas Bolle took John to court over occupancy of some land. However neighbours Robert Symons and John Kent attested Cowper had held the land for over two years.[3]

John Cowper died in 1602. By will he described himself as 'husbandman of Hensington'.[4] He names a brother, William Savage of North Leigh and a sister, Joan Spencer; these would be children of John Savage who died in 1557. Joan was married to Roger Spencer whose children were legatees of John Holowaye in 1585. John Cowper's three children survived him; the son John Cooper already mentioned, a daughter Alice, married to Richard Banting and an unnamed daughter married to Michael Nurse, a Woodstock butcher. Grandchildren were named John and George Cooper, Robert and Elizabeth Banting. Bequests, typical of a small landowner, were sums of money, livestock (mainly cattle) and measures of grain for family members. Servants received 12d above their wages. Son John Cooper was executor and overseers were Ralph Bradshaw, mercer of Woodstock, and Michael Nurse, John Cowper's son in law, who received a quarter of wheat as legacy and a bushel of wheat as payment for overseeing the will. Although written in July 1602 the will was was not proved until November 1605. Despite the modest bequests, John Cowper's estate was valued at £79.10s. He had made his wealth in agriculture because he did not marry into money, John Holowaye, his father in law, left bequests of only a few shillings or pence.

The Banting family

Cowper's son in law Richard Banting was a tanner by trade; living in Bladon in 1602 he later moved to live in Old Woodstock where his daughter Anne, described as a servant, married local miller, William Green. Unusually for the time, Anne Banting's baptism at Bladon in 1602, her marriage in 1624 and her burial at Wootton in 1666 are all recorded in parish registers. Richard Banting died in 1627 naming his son Robert and daughters Elizabeth Kilbie and Anne Green as legatees.[5] A child, registered as Richard Brenting, baptised and buried at Bladon in 1598 was probably another son of the family. The Bantings were not wealthy, living in a three-roomed house of hall, buttery and chamber. In his inventory Richard's goods were valued at just £17 with his working tools and tannery equipment accounting for £10 of the whole.

Signature of Richard Banting, tanner (d.1627), who married Alice Cooper.

At his burial in 1627 he was described as of Old Woodstock.

Michael Nurse, Cowper's son in law, can be traced in Nurse family documents as having married Anne Cooper of Hensington.[6] Michael was the youngest son of Richard and Margery Nurse and brother of Joan Nurse who married Ralph Bradshaw, the wealthy Woodstock mercer of the late 16th century.[7]

There are no probate documents for the Cooper family for forty-five years after 1602; but John Cooper appears frequently as witness, supervisor, executor and appraiser for residents of Hensington and was clearly a leading inhabitant. Presumably he carried on farming in Hensington throughout these years.

In the published version of the chamberlains' accounts the name John Cooper is indexed with an alias of John Pepper. The latter name appears regularly in Woodstock documents; John Pepper, a cooper by trade, was admitted freeman in 1616 and appears in inhabitants' lists. The supposition that he was also known as John Cooper is based on the rent rolls which show that in 1613 the tenant of a shop near the High Cross was named as Pepper Cooper (cooper); in 1614 the entry reads 'for his (Pepper's) shop'. At the same time in 1608 and again in 1614 John Cooper is listed as both owner and occupier of a tenement in Oxford Street.[8] After 1614 the names of both John Cooper and John Pepper appear in the chamberlains' accounts from time to time but never as 'Cooper, alias Pepper' or vice versa. Whereas the rent roll entries do not seem firm evidence for a possible alias, conversely by mid 17th century John Cooper had acquired the house occupied by John Pepper and bequeathed the premises to his sons Henry and George Cooper.

The will of John Cooper, son of John Cowper (d.1602) appears in 1647.[9] The neat, closely written, hand is probably that of the testator and if so shows some degree of education. Beginning with the usual statement of weakness of body but perfect remembrance, the will stands alone among Woodstock wills for the length and content of the religious preamble; twenty four lines in contrast to the usual three or four. Firstly John states his belief in one God in Trinity; he describes the creation of man in the form of Adam whose disobedience caused the misery of mankind and God's goodness in sending Christ to suffer for the forgiveness of men's sins.

He leaves his soul to the blessed Trinity, for cleansing of its 'horrible pollutions' confident that it will be presented unblameable at the Lord's coming on the last day to be reunited with his body in heaven and praise God along with others redeemed. With this emphasis on personal sin and intent to set all things in order, both spiritually and personally, this is clearly the will of a man with strong puritan beliefs and lifestyle. It gives perhaps the only example of religious zeal to be found in Woodstock wills and could indicate also the political trends of the Cooper family who became prominent in town government in the commonwealth period.

There is a further occurrence of the Cooper surname in the chamberlains' accounts; 'Mr. Cooper', a preacher, is paid for sermons in 1632 and 1637. It is a common surname and there is nothing to link the preacher to the Hensington family, but perhaps a man who included such a testament with his will could have preached a sermon or two?

Signature of John Cooper (d. 1647). The letter 'p' is written in the form indicating two missing letters 'er'.

John Cooper left ten shillings for the poor of Bladon and Hensington, and ten shillings for the preacher at his funeral with a request to remind the living of their mortality and pray with those attending the interment.

Robert, his son and executor had to see his body interred in Christian manner but he named no place of burial. However the burial of 'Mr. Cowper of Hensington' is recorded at Bladon on 3rd June 1648. His baptism is also recorded at Bladon in 1572 so he was aged 75 at his death. John's wife, Jane, who died in 1635 was also buried at Bladon.

John Cooper had several sons and states in his will his desire to preserve peace and unity between them. The eldest, also named John, was left household linen and such of his father's books as were useful to his profession; having left the area and fallen on hard times he received £4 annually from a house and yardland[10] in Hensington 'until restored to his former estate'. Second son, George Cooper, was left a life interest in the southern part of a house and close in Woodstock where Blundon lived and part of a house in Hensington where Edith Hollis lived,[11] with a garden and six stocks of bees provided that if George's brother John became destitute and returned to Woodstock he should have the Hensington house for habitation. George was also left the largest Bible. Son Henry Cooper was left the northern part of a house in Woodstock with use of a well in the close reverting to son Samuel if Henry died without heirs and similarly to youngest son William Cooper. A married daughter, Ann Tell, received 40s yearly from profits of the house in Hensington. The residue went to son Robert Cooper as executor.

The will provides a link with the Hollis family of Hensington. John Cooper, described as her landlord, was appointed executor of Edith Hollis' will.[12] In 1611 Walter Hollis, Edith's son, was found guilty in Woodstock court of thieving from William Bradshaw's shop and punished in the stocks for his wrongdoings. Anne Cooper, a servant of John Bradshaw and described as Hollis's girlfriend, was accused of receiving goods and punished alongside him.[13] Walter Hollis left town and his whereabouts were unknown in 1632 when his widowed mother died. She left him £5 in her will, but if not collected in ten years it went to the poor of Hensington. She left Anne Cooper 'a platter that Robert Spittle gave my child', perhaps a keepsake of Walter. There may have been a family link between Anne Cooper, whose mother lived in Barton, and the Coopers of Hensington.

John Cooper's carefully drawn will with its religious content and careful division of property shows a man firmly in control and anxious to provide for all his children whatever their estate. Unfortunately the will was not proved in the local Church Courts by executor Robert Cooper. Several other Woodstock wills were probated in the 1640's despite the civil war difficulties. During the commonwealth period the Church Courts did not function and all wills were proved before judges in the London Registry. In 1675, long after the executor's death, John Cooper's estate was administered by his grandson John, a city of London goldsmith.[14]

Robert Cooper is known to have lived in the house, near the High Cross and guildhall, which belonged to the Flye family in the first quarter of the 17th century.[15] This house, occupied by Blundon, was divided between George and Henry Cooper by their father's will. Robert had married Elizabeth, daughter of Saloman Flye and granddaughter of alderman William Flye.[16] There is reference in Robert's will to half of a house once occupied by Robert Flye, Elizabeth's brother. Robert Flye and Robert Cooper both applied for admission as Woodstock freemen in 1637.[17]

Though successful in business both in Woodstock and Hensington, Robert Cooper took an active part in Woodstock town affairs. He was chamberlain from 1652 to 1655 and again from 1657 to 1659 becoming an alderman on the death of Nicholas Mayott in January 1660. Cooper's election is not recorded at the chamberlains' audit. Mercer Alexander Johnson, married to Joan, sister of Elizabeth Cooper, held the office of chamberlain alongside Robert Cooper, and was promoted to alderman in 1657 on George Noble's death. With town clerk, John Williams, brother of Anne, Johnson's first wife, this small family group held considerable influence during the commonwealth and the Cooper's puritan upbringing may have fitted well into the stricter regime of those times. Robert Cooper however did not achieve the highest office of mayor as he died in March 1661.

An inventory dated 29th January 1662 describes Robert Cooper as an alderman of the borough but his goods show him to have worked as an ironmonger and smith while maintaining his interest in farming.[18] The appraisers, including brother in law Alexander Johnson, valued a thousand weight of iron and other ironwares in the shop or store at £60. A working shop housed anvil and bellows with other working tools and also contained fuel in the shape of wood and coal (one of the earliest references to the latter in Woodstock). On the husbandry side in Hensington there was hay worth £10; corn in a barn appraised at £50 and the same value of corn on the ground. Livestock included 3 cows, 6 horses and 100 sheep, the latter worth £30. Wagons and carts were appraised at £20. There was malt worth £40 on the premises and a cellar contained brewing equipment. Robert Cooper's house was of moderate size with hall, parlour, kitchen and shop all with chambers over. The highest valued household goods were brassware at £10 and linen, which included 24 pairs of sheets, at £17.

Alderman Robert Cooper's will, written on 7th March 1661, names the three sons and four daughters who survived him. Another son, Solomon Flie Cooper, died in August 1657 when a few days old. The will deals mainly with division of property between his sons and sums of money for his daughters; none of the children appear married at their father's death. Eldest son John received the largest bequest, a half of the late Robert Flye's house and £30 at the end of his apprenticeship. Second son Robert received the income from Benjamin Careing's house after sixteen years paying Jane Cooper £20 after a further four years. Son George Cooper received half of Blundons house, bequeathed to Robert's brother George by their father's will of 1647. George Cooper did not live to receive his bequest; his burial is recorded shortly after that of his father in 1661. George Cooper, brother of alderman Robert, was left 'meate, drinke and cloathes and washing and wringeing dureing his life'. Such phrases usually indicate relatives needing care due to illness or incapacity. Robert's daughters received their inheritance at thirty, a much later age than the usual eighteen or twenty-one; Elizabeth was left £60, Mary and Joan £50 each and Jane £30. The residue went to Elizabeth Cooper as widow and sole executrix. The will was proved by her on 22nd February 1662.

Widow Elizabeth Cooper died in 1704 outliving two more of her children; Robert who took over his father's ironmongery business, died in

1670 and Jane died in 1671.[19] Administration of Jane's estate was granted to her mother and an inventory was drawn up by Edmund Johnson, her cousin; the £50 legacy from her father and wearing apparel worth £2 were her only assets.[20]

Alderman Robert Cooper's brothers appear in a few Woodstock documents; the chamberlains' accounts describe the brothers Henry and William Cooper as bakers in 1625 and another brother, George Cooper, was paid 5s to carry refuse out of the town after the King's visit in 1627.

Henry was not named in his grandfather's will of 1602 so was probably born after that date. Described as a baker in 1625 he was admitted freeman in 1632. At the hearth tax in 1665 he was taxed on 2 hearths; not among the wealthier residents.[21] In the commonwealth period, when Robert Cooper was chamberlain, Henry became a common councillor holding office until 1662 when he was one of five councillors disfranchised by the King's Commissioners.[22]

Assuming that alderman Robert's son John remained in London where he was established as a goldsmith, the deaths of his sons George and Robert would have left the family without male heirs locally and the surname would have disappeared. The younger brothers Samuel and William Cooper, as residual legatees, would not have benefited from their father's 1647 will and probably sought a living away from Woodstock. However, Robert's brother Henry remained in the town.

Henry, then described as a cordwainer, died in 1669. His widow Anne administered his estate but there is no inventory valuation.[23] The Woodstock registers list two of Henry and Anne's children, Bartholomew baptised 1654 and Marie baptised and buried in 1659. For the purposes of family history the name Bartholmew is fortuitous; three further generations can be traced bearing this name and take the family into the nineteenth century.

Bartholomew Cooper, an innkeeper, made his will 1741.[24] Unfortunately, having only one son, he felt no need to identify him by christian name. The son received a watch and £10 in money with the residue going to Bartholomew's wife, also unnamed. However, parish registers list the baptism of Bartholomew, son of Bartholomew and Hester Cooper, on 23rd February 1723 and this must be the same family. The younger Bartholomew married Sarah Norman on 1st September 1742. They had several children, one of whom, Richard Cooper, married Elizabeth Graham in 1774 and this couple gave the name Bartholomew to their fourth son baptised on 20th September 1786.

In 1815 the latter Bartholomew married Sarah Verney but this couple raised only one child, George, baptised in Woodstock in the same year. However, William Cooper, the latter Bartholomew's brother may have been the same William whose seven children were baptised in Woodstock before 1826. This William probably married out of the parish; his wife's name was Sarah. William is described mainly as a breeches maker and once as a glover at his childrens' baptism entries. His burial is not recorded but his wife was probably the same Sarah buried in 1855 aged 70.[25]

If these latter assumptions are correct the Coopers might be considered the family with the longest association with Hensington and the town of Woodstock, covering nearly three hundred years from mid 16th to early 19th century.

References

1   ORO MSS. Wills (Oxon), 182:39.
2   ORO MSS. Wills (Oxon), 131/4/1.
3   WCBk, 80..
4   ORO MSS. Wills (Oxon), 11/2/53.
5   ORO MSS. Wills (Oxon), 11/2/53.
6   ORO MSS. Wills (Oxon), 47/2/2, 89/1/17.
7   See Family of Ralph Bradshaw.
8   WCA, 39, 57.
9   ORO MSS. Wills (Oxon), 14/2/3.
10 Yardland = a measure of land of a virgate or 30 acres (Collins).
11 Identified as next to the guildhall site, formerly property of the Flye family; VCH Oxon, xii, 357.
12 ORO MSS. Wills (Oxon), 131/5/23.
13 See Bradshaw family (Ralph).
14 ORO MSS. Wills (Oxon), 107:179, 14/2/3.
15 VCH Oxon, xii, 357.
16 See Flye family (included in Johnson family).
17 WCA, 165.
18 ORO MSS.Wills (Oxon), 13/4/12.
19 Woodstock burials register.
20 ORO MSS. Wills (Oxon), 296/3/56.
21 Weinstock, ORS Vol. 21.
22 WBM Council minutes – 1661 to 1670.
23 ORO MSS. Wills (Oxon), 78/2/17, 107:151.
24 ORO MSS. Wills (Oxon), 211.19, 122/5/16.
25 See family tree and Woodstock parish registers.

Fletcher and associated families

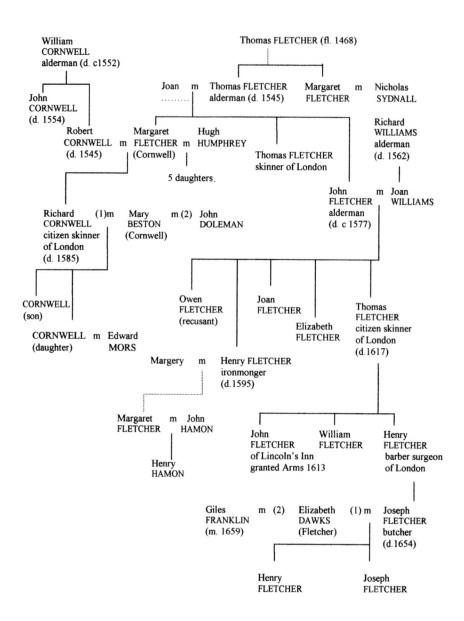

The Fletcher family of Woodstock

The surname dates back to John Fletcher who in 1395 was indicted in a Woodstock court for the murder of Thomas Burgeys.[1] For the Fletchers an inauspicious introduction to Woodstock; however John was later acquitted at his trial in Oxford.

It is uncertain whether John Fletcher can be linked to the next surname reference. A Woodstock rent roll of 1468[2] shows Thomas Fletcher paying 6d for a vacant plot and garden described as bordering William Faukener's house on the west, Wappenhams Lane to the east and stretching from Frog Lane to High Street along its length.[3] This plot is identified as the present day Fletcher's House and grounds, now The Oxfordshire Museum.

Sixty years later, in 1526, another Thomas Fletcher was paying 6d rent for a house on the site.[4] He was definitely related; a son or grandson of the above Thomas. There is some documentary information on Thomas Fletcher of 1526; a butcher and skinner by trade he became an alderman before 1535, the year he was town mayor.[5] The Fletchers had good connections within the town and surrounding area; Thomas's will appointed three overseers, William Cornwell, John Barnes and Richard Williams, all Woodstock aldermen; the family was also friendly with the Whittons, local gentry of Woodstock park.

Thomas's will of 1545 supplies much family background.[6] He left a wife, Joan, sons, John and Thomas, and daughter Margaret. Elder son, John, was bequeathed a house in Woodstock with garden and slaughter-house. These premises were the main family residence next to the present day Fletcher's House site. Younger son, Thomas, inherited a barn in Woodstock. Leases of Yarnton land were divided between the two sons. The alderman's wife, Joan, was left 'all lands, tenements, barns, gardens, leases and pastures' for her widowhood with residue described as 'money, plate, household stuff and cattle both in field and town'. This last bequest to go to her son Thomas if she re-marry. The will shows Thomas Fletcher to have been a considerable landowner with property both in

Woodstock and Yarnton. He acquired some of his land after Henry VIII's dissolution of the monasteries. Crown agents Richard Andrews and Leonard Chamberlain both lived in the Woodstock area and were responsible for distribution of monastic and church estates.[7]

Thomas Fletcher's daughter, Margaret, married Robert, son of alderman William Cornwell, their son Richard was left just 20s in his maternal grandfather's will.

The Cornwell family

The family's three generations cover the middle years of the 16th century. Alderman William Cornwell, earliest and most successful of the family, was mayor on several occasions from 1538.[8] William had two sons, Robert (d. 1545)[9] and John (d. 1554); his will, written in 1550 two years before probate, included a four-year annuity of ten shillings for Martin King, to be administered by executor John Cornwell.[10] At John's death in 1554 his widow, Joan, was charged to continue paying this annuity; Martin King was described as John Cornwell's natural brother.[11]

William Cornwell was a baker and brewer by trade;[12] in the early 16th century he acquired the site of present day 13-17 High Street and may have built a sizeable house there. By his will this property was subjected to a 6s 8d annual charge, administered by the town, for distribution to the poorest householders on Good Friday; the annuity later converted to a bread charity.[13] Another house, occupied by John Bruce, was left to William's widow for life reverting to grandson Richard Cornwell on her death. The bequest may have helped to fund Richard when he took an apprenticeship in London with his uncle Thomas Fletcher, lately of Woodstock, a member of the London guild of skinners. Richard is best remembered as founder of the grammar school in Woodstock; his generous bequest of £300 to the town provided school premises and schoolmaster's salary. Richard's widow Mary later provided money to purchase a schoolmaster's house at 10-12 Oxford Street. She and her second husband, John Doleman, set up a rent charge on property in Childrey, Bucks, to support the grammar school.[14] This annuity, known as Doleman's Charity, was collected by the town well into the 20th century for the support of local scholars.

In 1545 Margaret Cornwell faced the loss of her father, Thomas Fletcher, and her husband, Robert Cornwell. Both men wrote their wills on the same day, 24th May, suggesting they were visited by sudden illness;

epidemics of plague and viral diseases were common during much of the 16th century. Neither survived the illness; Thomas's will was proved in July and Robert's in October 1545. Although her mother was well provided by Thomas Fletcher's will and her brother, John Fletcher, took over his father's house and trade, Margaret herself received no legacy from her father. Her husband was worth only £8.13.4d on his death. Also she had her infant child, Richard Cornwell, to raise; his father left him only six silver spoons.

So Margaret re-married fairly soon, her second husband was yeoman Hugh Humphrey. Not resident in Woodstock, Hugh was perhaps visiting the family in 1546 when he and John Fletcher were called to witness the will of John Glover, innholder of the Crown.[15] Margaret and Hugh had several daughters; Richard Cornwell refers to five sisters in his 1585 will.[16]

Soon after his father's death John Fletcher married Joan Williams, daughter of Woodstock alderman Richard Williams who, in 1562, left money to the couple's five children; Owen, Harry (Henry), Joan, Elizabeth and a son unnamed.[17]

John Fletcher is traceable mainly in late 16th century probate documents; most notably he witnessed the will of Owen Whitton comptroller of Woodstock Park in 1554.[18] John's eldest son, Owen, was perhaps named after him. In 1558 John was described as alderman when witness to William Pyman's will[19] and in the same year was mayor of Woodstock, an office he held on seven occasions. There is no surviving will for John Fletcher and the date of his death is untraced; however his final term as mayor was 1575–6. In 1581 John's widow, Joan Fletcher, quitclaimed Fletchers House to Henry, her second son.[20]

John and Joan Fletcher's eldest son, Owen, left Woodstock and made his own adventurous way in the world. Born about 1553 when England was strongly protestant under Edward VI, Owen was raised during the strictly catholic times of Mary Tudor when perhaps he was influenced to follow the teachings of the Roman church. After matriculating at Trinity College, Oxford, in 1572 aged 19, Owen gained a Bachelor of Arts degree in 1575. In the next decade he became known for his religious views and gained notice as a recusant.[21] As a young man he would have led a dangerous life for his beliefs; Queen Elizabeth's agents were constantly seeking recusants and terrible punishments were practised, often ending in execution. Owen did not escape detection, in 1585 he was committed to London's Gatehouse prison. He is next listed among men who went over to the seminary at Rheims in 1591 and on 21st May 1592 he was ordained a priest in Laon. The following year he returned to England where a recusant, Thomas Sleepe, reported he spoke to Fletcher, a preacher at Clerkenwell. There were Fletchers living in Clerkenwell in the later 16th century;[22] perhaps this branch of the family provided shelter and safety for Owen. A further spell in prison ended on 31st December 1598 when he escaped with another seminary priest, Martin Lister, from the Marshalsea. There is reference to a priest named Fletcher at the English College in Rome in 1604 but no further references to Owen in London. It is just possible that an entry in the burial register of St. James, Clerkenwell, in 1636 refers to him although it reads 'Owen Fletcher a poor *woman*'. Owen would have been aged 82 that year.[23]

It is impossible to guess the effect of Owen's actions on his family in Woodstock. It is unlikely he ever returned to his birthplace; if disinherited from the family home on his father's death the house would revert to his brother Henry, an ironmonger. One possible reaction to Owen's notoriety is contained in the 1585 will of his cousin Richard Cornwell, the grammar school founder. His bequests to his three unmarried sisters contained provisos that they must 'marry such sort as fear God and be not papist' in order to collect their £10 legacies on their marriage days. Richard, a wealthy member of the London skinners' guild, was well established in the capital, for his family's sake he might have thought it advisable to disassociate himself from his cousin's beliefs. In 1585 Owen was in the Gatehouse prison.

Joan Fletcher, John's widow, probably lived with her son Henry until her death. She was alive in 1592 when mentioned in the will of widow, Floraunce Condall.[24] Henry's name appears as common councillor in the borough constitution of 1580; his only action of note was signatory to the 1581 memorandum which disfranchised George Whitton of Woodstock Park. By 1590 Henry had progressed to junior chamberlain.[25] An iron-monger by trade and freeman of the borough, he was a frequent user of the portmoot court and suitor in eleven actions between 1588 and 1595. In addition he often served as juror and pledged bail both for plaintiffs and defendants.[26]

Henry's wife Margery, birth surname unknown, lived in the family home for many years after his death; she is named on a list of Woodstock widows in October 1619.[27] Seemingly by 1609 she had leased parts of the premises to alderman Thomas Browne, who gradually acquired the complete site. She may have regretted this action later; in 1617 she appeared in the portmoot court claiming she still owned three parts of the seven messuages he had leased. However, her claim was over-ruled when Browne produced records in parchment with the mayoral seal. There are no wills for Henry and Margery Fletcher and therefore no record of any children of their marriage but in 1595, the year of Henry's death, a marriage was registered at Wootton of Margaret Fletcher to John Hamon.[28] A son, Henry, was baptised in April 1596; the couple was then described as of Old Woodstock.[29] If Margaret was the daughter of Henry and Margery it would have been convenient for her to marry as soon as she had no father to support her.

Elizabeth and Joan, daughters of John and Joan Fletcher, have not been traced but may well have married into other influential Woodstock families. Their younger brother, Thomas, unnamed in grandfather Richard Williams' will, was apprenticed to his cousin Richard Cornwell in

Fletcher family Coat of Arms granted in 1613 to Thomas Fletcher, skinner of London, son of John Fletcher of Woodstock. Crest: a fleur de lys or pellettês Gules, a chevron argent between three laurel leaves of the second, on a canton per bend sinister vert and azure 3 fleurs de lis or between eight besants.

London and admitted freeman of the Skinners' Company in 1585, the year Cornwell died.[30] Richard left him £10 in his will.[31]

Shortly before his death Thomas Fletcher applied for a Grant of Arms and this was awarded on 26th April 1613. The Grant was made to 'Thomas Fletcher of London, gent, son and heir of John Fletcher of Woodstock, Oxfordshire (descended out of Lanc.) and to John Fletcher his son'.[32] In 1617 Thomas followed Richard Cornwell's example leaving money to the townspeople of Woodstock; an annual £12 to provide £4 for a schoolmaster's salary with the remainder to pay for sermons and aid for the poor.[33] As early as 1618 the town used 3s of his money to buy a coat for a baseborn child.[34] The chamberlains' accounts note that from 1642 the bequest was collected annually from Skinners' Hall in London; there are many references to the poor receiving 'Mr. Fletcher's money'. Woodstock had puritan sympathies in early 17th century and records also show many payments to preachers for delivering the sermons.

The chamberlains' accounts refer to an intended memorial to Richard Cornwell and Thomas Fletcher in acknowledgement of their generosity to Woodstock. It was to take the form of a framed table of verses in gilt letters. John Cooper was paid for gilding and 'bewtifyinge them'; the verses were bound and sent to Mr. John Fletcher for approval in 1619.[35]

The Fletcher surname might have died out following Margery's death in 1619 had not Joseph Fletcher of London taken up an 8-year apprenticeship with Richard Reade, a Woodstock butcher. His indenture is entered in the portmoot court book of September 1619; Joseph is described as 'son of Henry Fletcher, barber chirurgeon of the city of London'.[36]

In 1627 and again in 1629 the chamberlains accounted for wining and dining 'Mr. Fletcher's sonnes of London' when they visited the town. Their first visit cost only 16d for wine but on the second occasion they received 2 quarts of sack and a quart of white wine costing 3s. A footnote to the published accounts identifies these men as William and Henry Fletcher, sons of the town's benefactor.[37] Henry must have been the father of Joseph the apprentice butcher.

Joseph may have married a local girl named Elizabeth, the event unrecorded due to Woodstock's missing registers; but another distinct possibility is that he was the same Joseph Fletcher who married Elizabeth Dawks at Banbury on 10th November 1639.[38] The bride's christian name matches that of his known wife and by that date he was out of his apprenticeship and well established in trade.

Joseph became a freeman in 1627, the year his apprenticeship ended.[39]

Following his admission he is not mentioned in chamberlains' accounts until 1647 when he was supplying wooden posts for the town.[40] He may have lived away for a few years, perhaps in Banbury; however he is named as debtor in a baker's will of 1641.[41] In 1650 he was allowed to trade from his house and display his wares in the street for 20s a year.[42] Also he served four years as churchwarden until his death in 1654.[43]

In 1649 Joseph took a corporation lease of Muncks Mead, part of the town's meadow or Ley Poole. [44] Muncks Mead had been let to alderman Bartholomew Love; other meads were leased to alderman Thomas Glover and town clerk John Williams. In the later years of his life Joseph Fletcher may have dealt in stabling and hiring of horses in addition to the butchery trade which would explain his need for the meadow lease. In 1647 he charged 6d to Edmund Hiorne for horse hire.[45] After Joseph's death his son, Henry, detained and refused to return two horses, the goods of his late father.

The churchwardens' accounts list £1.1s due to Joseph Fletcher's widow in 1654. Elizabeth Fletcher's administration accounts reveal that Joseph died following an accident with a horse, lying sick for a while at an inn and paying them 10s for his care. He may have returned to Woodstock before he died in 1654; his burial on 13th April is among the earliest entries in the parish registers. When her accounts were exhibited in 1661 the widow's expenditure included £1 for deodand paid as redemption for a horse. This tax was leviable on any object deemed to have caused a man's death. 'Deodand' translates as 'the hand of God' i.e. accidental death not by the hand of man. The tax was normally payable to the crown but must have been demanded by parliament at that date.[46]

The opening clause of Elizabeth Fletcher's 1661 administration is worded 'at present the wife of (blank) Franklin, of Woodstock aforesaid, barber'; the phrase was then crossed through.

Elizabeth was already the wife of Giles Franklin; they had married on 10th January 1659 in Woodstock. Five years of widowhood seems a respectable interval before re-marriage so it is unclear why this was not acknowledged. Elizabeth was left with a deficit of £23 following her husband's unexpected death; after all the expenses involved she must have been in some financial difficulty. Her second marriage ended with the death of Giles Franklin in July 1665, her own burial is registered in November 1683.[47]

Joseph and Elizabeth Fletcher had two sons, Henry and Joseph. Both lived in Woodstock, gaining admission as freemen in the 1660's.[48] In 1658 George Gregory, gent, of Woodstock left £40 and Richard Scurrier's house to George, son of Henry and Dorothy Fletcher.[49] In 1661 his widow, Dorothy Gregory, named Dorothy Fletcher as her niece.[50] However, this branch of the Fletcher family does not feature in Woodstock parish registers.

Thus ends the story of the Fletchers. They prospered from the time of Thomas, tenant of the corner plot in 1468, through the influential years of Thomas (d.1545) and his son John, mayor on seven occasions. The family was lauded for the benefactions of Richard Cornwell and Thomas Fletcher, the city of London skinners, but gradually dwindled in influence from the time of Joseph, apprentice butcher, disappearing from town documents in mid-17th century.

References

1   *ORS. LIII*, 154 Sessions of the Peace in the reign of Richard II. E Kimball.
2   WBM 83/1 *f 15.*
3   Present day – Wappenhams = Browns Lane, Frog Lane = Harrisons Lane & High Street = Park Street.
4   *VCH Oxon*, xii, 350.
5   Marshall – List of mayors.
6   ORO MSS. Wills (Oxon), 179:66.
7   Taylor, RF, Probate debts & credits in the Woodstock community 1530 – 1700 (unpublished).
8   Marshall – List of mayors.
9   ORO MSS. Wills (Oxon), 179:96.
10 ORO MSS. Wills (Oxon), 180:122v.
11 ORO MSS. Wills (Oxon),) 162/3/1.
12 *VCH Oxon*, xii, 360.
13 *VCH Oxon*, xii, 420.
14 *VCH Oxon*, xii, 416.
15 ORO MSS. Wills (Oxon), 179:166v.
16 WBM B97 – copy of will.
17 ORO MSS. Wills (Oxon), 184:44.
18 ORO MSS. Wills (Oxon), 180:251.
19 ORO MSS. Wills (Oxon), 183:54v.
20 *VCH Oxon*, xii, 350. Quitclaim = release, discharge or relinquish title or claim to (Collins).
21 'Recusant'. One who refuses to accept the teachings of the Church of England.
22 e.g. a boy, Thomas Fletcher, was baptised at St.James, Clerkenwell, in 1586.
23 (Unpublished) research on Owen Fletcher by Mary Hodges, tutor of Woodstock local history group.
24 ORO MSS. Wills (Oxon), 10/5/49.
25 WBM B81 *f 13.*

26 *WCBk passim.*
27 WBM B 96 Inhabitants' lists.
28 Wootton marriage register.
29 Wootton baptism register.
30 Records of Skinners Company of London, Guildhall library.
31 WBM B97 – copy will of Richard Cornwell.
32 Records of Harlean Society 1915 Grants of Arms (research by Mary Hodges).
33 WBM B97 – summary of will.
34 *WCA*, 72 – baseborn = illegitimate.
35 *WCA*, 73, 74.
36 WBM B78/3 *f 167.*
37 WBM B78/3 *f 167.*
38 ORO Banbury marriage index.
39 *WCA*, 115.
40 *WCA*, 207.
41 ORO MSS. Wills (Oxon), 47/4/13.
42 *WCA*, 228.
43 WBM CW 83 *f 45.*
44 Previous researcher left note 'date – two days after execution of Chas.I; reads ...in the year of our Lord God 1649'.
45 *WCA*, 209.
46 ORO MSS. Wills (Oxon), 297/2/36.
47 Woodstock burial register.
48 WBM Council minutes 1661–1700.
49 PRO PROB. 11/289.184.
50 ORO MSS. Wills (Oxon), 26/4/11.

Glover and associated families

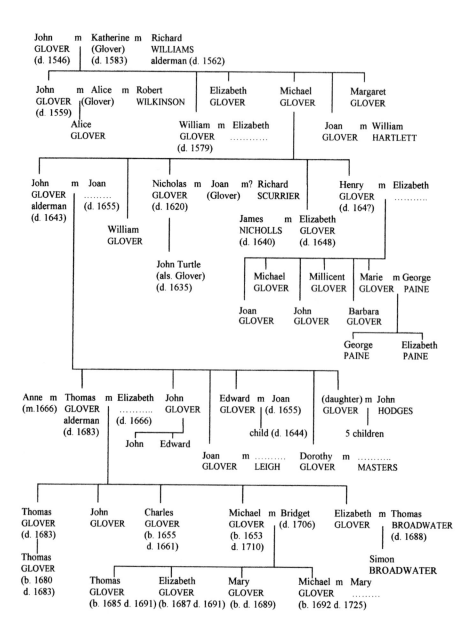

The Glover family

For two hundred years the Glover family made a contribution to social and corporate activities in Woodstock. The surname does not occur in a 1468 rent roll[1] but by mid-16th century the family was well established, occupying one of the foremost inns, the Crown, (now 9–11 Market Place), where they remained for two centuries.[2]

In 1546 John Glover, a shoemaker, made his last will and testament.[3] The will detailed some family members – his wife, Katherine, and three sons, John, William and Michael. There are references to daughters but only one, Elizabeth, is named in the will. John bequeathed the Crown Inn to his wife for life reverting to their eldest son John on her death, to sons William and Michael in turn and then to the daughters. Katherine was sole executrix; she later married alderman Richard Williams, appointed overseer in her husband's will.

Katherine owned the Crown until her death in 1583, but may have turned over management to one her sons on her re-marriage. The chantry quit rent of 18d was paid in 1598[4] and 1601[5] but tenants' names are unrecorded.

John Glover, a shoemaker, eldest son of John and Katherine died in 1559;[6] the late 1550s were noted for bad harvests and high mortality and John, a young man, possibly fell victim to one of the epidemics which swept the country in those years. He married after 1546 and had one daughter, Alice, named after his wife. He had not inherited the Crown as his mother was still living; however he rented part of the common pool of Woodstock, usually reserved for aldermen or councillors, and left this lease to his wife.[7]

John left small legacies to four family servants. One of these, Robert Wilkinson, a shoemaker apprenticed to Glover, subsequently married John's widow, Alice. She was soon widowed again when Robert Wilkinson died in 1568.[8] Perhaps she was the 'widow Wilkinson' who owed rent to the town in 1591.[9]

William Glover, second son of John and Katherine, also predeceased his mother and would not have inherited the Crown Inn. His widow, Elizabeth, took letters of administration to his estate on 3rd July 1579.[10]

Katherine Williams died in 1583. Her will reveals much useful information for family historians as well as some complexities.[11] Confusingly she mentioned three daughters named Joan; certainly one of these, John Fletcher's wife, was a daughter of the first marriage of Richard Williams, Katherine's second husband, who died in 1562.[12] Another Joan (maybe a daughter of Katherine's first marriage) was probably married to William Hartlett, a servant of Florance Condall who lodged with the Williams family;[13] Joan Hartlett and her daughter Elizabeth were legatees. The third Joan, described as Katherine's daughter, is also mentioned in Richard Williams' will, but not by her given name. She married John Saunders of Kidlington and there were six children, including a girl named Joan. Possibly Katherine wrongly described Joan Saunders as her daughter really meaning granddaughter.

Under the terms of his father's will Michael Glover, the only son to outlive his mother, inherited the Crown Inn on her death.[14] In 1580 Michael was listed as one of three bakers licenced to trade in the town.[15] He was also licensed as victualler at the Sessions court in December 1595[16] and his name appears on rent rolls of 1598 and 1601. Katherine left him property in Woolmarket Street that possibly became his business premises. His eldest son, John, took over the Crown before his father's death. There are no probate documents for Michael; his name disappears from town records after 1601.

Michael Glover had five children, John, William, Nicholas, Henry and Elizabeth. John was the most successful; once admitted as a freeman he swiftly became a common councillor, chamberlain, alderman and, on five occasions, mayor of the town.

William, a Woodstock freeman from 1602, did not attain any office in the town.[17] Rent rolls show that he lived in Cooperyware market in 1598,[18] but in 1609 and 1613 the property was referred to as 'lately' his, suggesting he died before 1609.

Nicholas Glover, third son of Michael, a freeman from 1612,[19] was licensed as victualler before 1608.[20] He lived in Oxford Street in 1608 and in Woolmarket Street in 1613.[21] The chief references to Nicholas in town documents concern his fathering of John, illegitimate son of Margaret Turtle.[22] The chamberlains' accounts show the boy, partly funded by the town, was fostered by several local families. John Turtle eventually went to the almshouses where he died in 1635.[23] Woodstock documents show arrangements for the raising of several baseborn children; the parents were summoned to court and bound to make regular payments towards upkeep. The arrangements for John Turtle seem particularly well documented and may reflect the status of the Glover family within the town.

Nicholas, a licensed victualler, died in 1620.[24] His widow, Joan, wound up his estate in that year and for a time was licensed as victualler herself, running her late husband's alehouse.[25] Nicholas had died owing £10 to his eldest brother, John, who pursued the debt in court eventually receiving a large quantity of the widow's goods as payment.[26] This action seems harsh; John Glover must have been in better circumstances as owner of the Crown than his recently widowed sister in law. Did animosity arise between John and Nicholas because the base child had brought shame to the family? In later Glover family wills Joan and Richard Scurrier's family received small legacies.[27] Maybe Joan was the re-married widow of Nicholas.

Henry Glover, fourth son of Michael, moved from Woodstock to live in Banbury.[28] Henry, his wife, Elizabeth, and family feature in the wills of James and Elizabeth Nicholls of Woodstock. Elizabeth, Henry's sister, left bequests to each of his six children in 1648. Henry died between 1640 and 1648.

Elizabeth Glover, only daughter of Michael, married baker James Nicholls. They ran an apparently successful business. James died in 1640 with goods valued at £149 and £86 due on bonds.[29] At her death in 1648 Elizabeth ordered that 20 dozen of bread and 10 dozen of cakes be distributed to the poor as she was carried out of the house for burial.[30] Establishing a bread charity was the more usual way to help the poor, but this generous bequest was intended solely for Elizabeth's contemporaries. Her inventory value was under £60. James and Elizabeth Nicholls apparently had no children, perhaps explaining their bequests to the Scurrier family.

John, eldest son of Michael Glover, both a baker and innholder was very actively involved with Woodstock town business and thus the best documented. A common councillor by 1601; he was elected chamberlain in 1608[31] and alderman in 1611.[32] The next year he was chosen to be mayor, an office he held on 5 occasions. His name appears regularly on probate documents of the 1610s to 1630s. As an appraiser he valued many inventories, particularly for notable townspeople such as Henry Rudgate, sergeant at mace.[33]

The Crown inn often entertained important visitors to Woodstock. In May 1621 the borough Recorder, Sir James Whitelock, held a licensing sessions there when some local difficulty arose between the mayor, John Glover, and local JP Jerome Kyte.[34] Sir James regularly visited Woodstock, often consulting on legalities in the portmoot court. The chamberlains' accounts record the expenses of his hosts; John Glover claimed 12s for one visit in 1622.

Accounts of the 1620s and 30s contain references to visiting preachers who were wined and dined on sack and claret at the inn. One of these, John Hodges, married John Glover's daughter. The Hodges later removed to Leicestershire when John obtained a living there.[35]

From the administration clause of John's inventory we learn that his wife was named Joan.[36] The couple had 6 children. In 1608, a year of food shortages in the town, inhabitants were called to declare the size of their households and what stores of grain they held: one entry reads 'John Glover, baker, has 9 persons in his house and bakes weekly 2 quarters of meal'.[37] The 9 persons would include both the growing family and servants.

Compared to some Woodstock inhabitants John had few dealings in property. However in 1638 he paid 30s to lease a large property in Hoggerill (now Hoggrove) Hill and this became his family's main residence.[38]

John died in 1643; an inventory of his goods and property totalled £201.[39] The Crown inn's rooms and furnishings are described in detail; visitors could stay in chambers named 'Crown', 'Little', 'White Hart', 'Rose', 'Green' or 'Star'. In addition the inn had a parlour, kitchen, three butteries, brewhouse, cockloft (attic), wheat loft and a 'new building'.

Joan Glover, John's widow, made her will in 1650, naming all but one of her six children, Thomas, John, Edward, Joan, Dorothy and a daughter described as the wife of John Hodges.[40]

Edward Glover, third son of John and Joan and executor to Joan's will, was left the residue of her estate and the Hoggerill Hill lease reverting to her grandson Michael, youngest son of Thomas, on Edward's death. There are few mentions of Edward Glover in Woodstock documents; however, admitted freeman in 1647,[41] he was paying £1.10s rent for the woolbeam in 1652.[42]

Thomas Glover, eldest son of John and Joan, was admitted freeman in 1631, elected chamberlain in 1648, and alderman in 1658.[43] He seems to have ridden out the changes in the council during the commonwealth period. In July 1662 after the restoration the King's Commissioners removed several common councillors as unfit to govern[44] and Thomas was appointed mayor in place of Alexander Johnson.[45]

Thomas was taxed on 8 hearths in the 1662 levy.[46] This figure would equate well with the rooms of the Crown inn described in the inventory of John Glover in 1643.[47]

After 1653 Thomas Glover's family can be traced in parish registers. They record the baptisms of two sons, Michael in 1653 and Charles in 1655. Another two sons and a daughter, not in the baptism registers, were probably born before 1653. Elizabeth Glover, wife of Thomas and mother of all his children, died in 1666. The same year a Thomas Glover was married in Bladon church but his wife's name was not recorded. Probably this a record of his second marriage; the wife mentioned in his will was named Anne.

Thomas died in 1683. He made his will on 28th September describing himself as 'aged and weak in body'.[48] He had outlived his father (John d.1643) by forty years and had several grandchildren; he could have been in his late 70s or early 80s.[49] 1683 was a very sad year for the Glovers; three generations died in that year. Woodstock registers note the burials of Thomas Glover's son, Thomas, in February and his grandson, also Thomas, in September, just one month before his grandfather.

Signatures of three generations of the Glover family; John (d. 1643) signs as mayor, Thomas (d. 1683) an alderman and Michael (d. 1710).

Michael Glover, Thomas's youngest son, inherited the Crown. Apart from the inn, Thomas's only notable legacy was £10 for his grandson, Simon Broadwater, son of his only daughter Elizabeth who married Thomas Broadwater, a newcomer to the town.[50] Probably Michael was well established as innkeeper when his father died because Thomas's inventory describes household goods in one chamber only.[51] It was common practice to allot one or two rooms in a house for use by elderly parents.

Before his father's death Michael Glover added to the Hoggerill Hill property, paying 13s 4d for a sixty year lease of premises adjoining the original house, in tenure of Hugh Jones, in 1679.[52] Interestingly the lease described Michael as a goldsmith; a more profitable trade than that of baker traditionally followed by his family since early in the century.

Michael Glover's family is fully recorded in Woodstock registers. Four children were baptised but only Michael, the youngest son born 1692, survived. Michael's wife, Bridget, is documented thus in the churchwardens' accounts:[53]

25th May 1684 'Agreed by ye Minister and Churchwardens that whereas Bridgett the wife of Michael Glover did presumptiously intrude her selfe into ye seat next ye Earle of Lichfields without being placed there by ye church wardens or having either theirs or ye ministers consent for soe doeing she ye said Bridget Glover be henceforth discharged from sitting any more there and Mrs. Hartford placed in that seat (signed by Humphrey Prideaux, John Brotherton, Benjamin Johnson, rector and churchwardens).

The Earl of Lichfield, descendent of Sir Henry Lee, was one of the nobility and gentry taking an interest in town affairs following the restoration. It was the mayor's privilege to arrange seating in the church and the Earl would have been allotted a more favourable position than ordinary townsfolk. Why was Mrs. Hartford allowed to sit next to him in preference to Bridget Glover?

Bridget Glover died in 1706 and Michael in 1710.[54]

In 1718 Michael Glover, only surviving son of Michael and Bridget, sold the Crown inn to Charles and Merrick Jenkins and in 1725 was probably living on Hoggerill Hill.[55] However he may have remained as innkeeper after the sale. His inventory drawn in 1725, describes a large house with rooms lavishly furnished but contains features which could equally appertain to an inn.[56] The premises include a brewhouse, old and new cellars, wine cellar, two kitchens, spence, parlour, dining room, yellow room, a gallery with staircase, rooms over both kitchens – one called the blue room, a red chamber, three bedrooms and 4 garrets. The dining room contained 6 tables and 10 leather chairs; prints, maps and a landscape ('landskip') adorned the walls. The wine cellar contained '7 dozen of wine' with 4 gallons of brandy and 3 bottles of canary wine and sack; another cellar held 2 hogsheads of mild beer. The brewhouse contained all the utensils for regular use. If all these features were situate in the house on Hoggerill Hill then the Glovers were living in grand style.

Thomas Hearne, in his calendar of social events of the early 18th century [57] writes:

22 March 1725… "Yesterday very early in the morning, one Glover, a lusty man about 6 ft high, a little more than 40 years of age, and a lissom person, who bore good character and kept the Crown Inn at Woodstock was found dead upon the road somewhere about Begbroke on his way to Woodstock having been at Oxford the day before in the afternoon to bespeake some wine of Mr. Bradgate at the Three Tuns Tavern in Oxford, who served him with the wine. Bradgate and he dranck a pint of wine apiece after which Glover called upon one Robert Matthews, uncle to his wife, and keeper of the Bocardo prison in Oxford where, 'tis said, he drank some ale and brandy which disordered him, I suppose, and it being withall a very dark night it might be the occasion of his death".

Michael Glover's burial is registered at Woodstock on 24th March 1725. Thomas Hearne seemingly attended the funeral. He writes further:

25th March (Ladyday) 1725… "The said Glover's wife is a jolly and very hand-some woman. I am told Glover went out of Oxford pretty soon in the evening, that a dead horse, happening to lye in the road above Begbroke, his own horse thereupon startled and pitching him upon his head in a cart rut, broke his neck."

This tragic death abruptly ends the Glover's association with Woodstock. Michael's widow, Mary, was left with the family's accumulated wealth and a grand house but apparently no children. The couple may not have been married very long, Michael was only 33 years of age at his death (Hearne had suggested 40). His burial is the final entry for the surname in the parish registers. However, Hearne says that Mary Glover was a jolly and handsome woman and it is to be hoped she soon found happiness with a new husband and family.

References

1   WBM, B83
2   *VCH Oxon,* xii, 354.
3   ORO MSS. Wills (Oxon), 179:166.
4   WBM B96 *f 87.*
5   WBM B96 *ff 4,5.*
6   ORO MSS. Wills (Oxon), 183:310.
7   *WCA* and see Rent rolls WBM 96.
8   ORO MSS. Wills (Oxon), 184:379.
9   WBM B81 *f 13.*
10 ORO MSS. Wills (Oxon), 186:77.
11 ORO MSS. Wills (Oxon), 156/1/13.
12 ORO MSS. Wills (Oxon), 184:44.
13 ORO MSS. Wills (Oxon), 10/5/49.
14 ORO MSS. Wills (Oxon), 179:166.
15 WBM B82.
16 *WCBk,* 124.
17 WBM B81 *f 19.*
18 WBM B96 *f 87.*
19 WBM B81 *f 25.*

20 WBM B78/2 *f 18.*

21 *WCA*, 33, 40.

22 WBM B78/2 *f 17.*

23 *WCA*, 27, 158.

24 ORO MSS. Wills (Oxon), 80/1/30.

25 WBM B78/3 *ff 222, 225v.*

26 WBM B78/3 *f 195.*

27 ORO MSS. Wills (Oxon), 47/4/13, 47/4/23.

28 ORO MSS. Wills (Oxon), 47/4/23.

29 ORO MSS. Wills (Oxon), 47/4/23.

30 ORO MSS. Wills (Oxon), 47/4/23.

31 WBM B81 *f 22.*

32 *WCA*, 233.

33 ORO MSS. Wills (Oxon), 55/2/44.

34 WBM B78/3 *f224v.*

35 ORO MSS. Wills (Oxon), 47/4/23.

36 ORO MSS. Wills (Oxon), 297/3/61.

37 WBM B78/2 *f 58v.*

38 *WCA*, 176.

39 ORO MSS. Wills (Oxon), 297/3/61.

40 PRO PROB. 11/248.

41 *WCA*, 207.

42 WBM B7/19.

43 *WCA*, 233.

44 *VCH Oxon*, xii, 374.

45 WBM Council Minutes 1661 to 1670 *f 4.*

46 *Weinstock*, 21.

47 ORO MSS. Wills (Oxon), 297/3/61.

48 ORO MSS. Wills (Oxon), 27/4/23.

49 WBM B96 (Muster Roll of adult males 1626).

50 Broadwater family in parish registers from 1677.

51 ORO MSS. Wills (Oxon), 27/4/23.

52 WBM Indentures B69/1/7.

53 Ox.Arch DD Par Woodstock C12. Churchwardens' accounts 1603 to 1702.

54 Woodstock Parish Registers.

55 *VCH Oxon,* xii, 354.

56 ORO MSS. Wills (Oxon), 166/4/9.

57 *OHS Hearne's Collections*, I, viii, 349.

Johnson and associated families

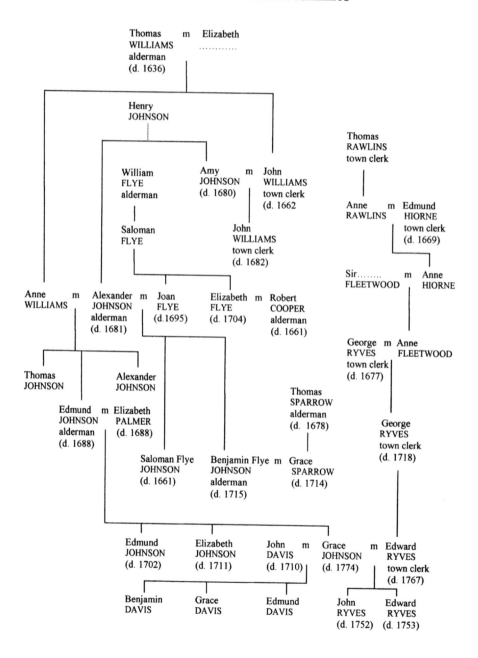

The Johnson family of Woodstock

In the late 16th and early 17th centuries the Bradshaw family apparently had a monopoly of the mercery trade in Woodstock. Ralph Bradshaw died in 1606 with estate valued over £400 and his sons, John and William, died as young men in 1614 and 1616 respectively.[1] A substantial gap had to be filled for Woodstock folk to enjoy the wide range of goods previously supplied by the Bradshaws. Incomer Thomas Woodward, mercer, was admitted freeman in 1619[2] but a decade later there was sufficient trade for two such establishments and in 1628 Alexander Johnson, a young mercer, was admitted freeman of Woodstock.[3]

The Johnson surname appears in town documents from around 1590. Henry Johnson, a suitor in portmoot court actions of 1590s,[4] was named as resident until 1608, but deleted from later inhabitants' lists.[5] Edward Johnson, tailor, was admitted in 1622 and listed as freeman from 1623.[6] Possibly he and Alexander were brothers, sons of Henry Johnson. The two younger Johnsons seem initially to have concentrated on trading; neither figured largely in town records of the period.

Probate documents provide a first clue to the Johnsons' eventual success. In his will of 1636 alderman Thomas Williams mentioned his daughter Anne, married to Alexander Johnson, and their young son, Thomas Johnson.[7] The Williams family had been established in Woodstock for about a century with each generation producing an alderman. Alexander's marriage into one of the foremost families was followed by his first appointment to office; he became constable in 1637. The next year he was chosen churchwarden, holding this office at intervals until 1646. Thereafter he signed the churchwardens' accounts yearly until 1662.[8] In 1639 John Williams, son of alderman Thomas, became second churchwarden and the brothers in law shared the post again in 1641. Thereafter their careers in town government followed a similar course.

Alexander was a common councillor before 1645, the year he was chosen as junior chamberlain.[9] The same year John Williams took over from Edmund Hiorne as town clerk.[10] The appointment lasted throughout the commonwealth period pointing to the political beliefs of Johnson's in laws. Alexander was senior chamberlain from 1651 until 1657 when a vacancy for alderman arose on the death of George Noble and he was duly elected. His next promotion was mayoralty in 1658/9 and again in 1661/2.[11] However, after the restoration of the monarchy, the King's commissioners arrived in the town in 1662 and, under act of parliament, ousted town clerk John Williams, along with mayor Alexander Johnson and others of the common council as being unfit to govern.[12] This marked the end of Alexander's career in town government; he took no further part in council affairs.

Anne and Alexander Johnson had several children, Thomas, their eldest son, was named in the will of his grandfather, Thomas Williams, in 1636. Due partly to fewer wills surviving from the commonwealth period only a scatter of probate documents include the Johnson family as witnesses, appraisers etc. The 1662 will of John Williams, lately town clerk, mentions his brother in law, Alexander Johnson, but not his sister Anne, Alexander's wife, who had died before that date.[13] Alexander Johnson's second wife was Joan Flye.

The Flye family

The Flyes were resident in Woodstock by 1589. William Flye, described variously as woolman or glover by trade, appeared regularly as juror in Portmoot and sessions courts.[14] He married twice; his first wife has not been traced but before 1595 he married Ann, daughter of weaver Michael Fauxe, a common councillor. In his 1595 will Fauxe left the couple a house occupied by Hugh Hammon, pewterer, in Beefmarket Street.[15] In an indenture of 1611 the house is described as given to William and Anne Flye on their marriage.[16] By early 17th century William had acquired a small portfolio of Woodstock properties including a house in High street (also known as Parkgate street), three cottages between Hoggerill hill and Edmund Hiorne's house on the east. His most valuable property, lately purchased from the Yeate family of Witney, was a house and shop next to the guildhall occupied by Edmund Rudgate, a shoe-maker and sergeant at mace. In 1611 William and Anne made over this and other properties by settlement to Saloman Flye, described as their only son.[17] In 1613 Saloman was still paying rent for some prop-erties but had sold others to William Dunford, yeoman of Woodstock, only days after receiving the settlement from his parents.[18] Although unable to sign his name, William Flye clearly

7 Market Place, Woodstock, built by Alexander Johnson in 1668. The gabled frontage is typical of 17th century houses.

had some business ability and became an alderman and mayor in 1618.[19] His death is not recorded but his name disappears from town documents after 1623. Saloman Flye died relatively young in 1616, leaving three children, Robert, Elizabeth and Joan.[20]

Despite the upheavals of the civil war and commonwealth period the local mercery trade still flourished. By 1668 Alexander Johnson was sufficiently wealthy to build or rebuild his house now 7 Market Place, one of very few in the town still showing the 17th century frontage. His initials AJ are carved on the street side of the house.[21]

In spite of removal from town office Alexander prospered and lived to enjoy the luxury of his new house. The inventory to his 1681 will lists six rooms; a great chamber, best chamber, hall with chamber over, kitchen, buttery and malt house. The list of mercery ware is not so comprehensive as that of John Bradshaw's over half a century earlier, but Woodstock residents could still buy woollen cloth, serge, linen, sacking, hair cloth and other basic materials. The presence of the royal court at Woodstock manor, together with the trade it brought, was greatly missed by Woodstock residents following the civil war. However, there were still local gentry and in the late 17th century both men and women dressed extravagantly. The wealthy could buy their silks, stockings, silver lace, galloons (fancy trimmings) and other haberdashery at Johnson's shop. Grocery wares were available but the shop obviously concentrated on the clothing trade, this stock accounting for about three-quarters of the shop goods, valued at nearly £500. The total inventory value was £702 including debts owing to the shop of just under £200.[22]

The burial of Anne Johnson, Alexander's first wife, is not recorded. His two youngest children, Benjamin and Saloman, were of his second marriage to Joan; her surname Flye was included as a given name. Saloman Flye Johnson, was baptised and died in 1661. Alexander's eldest son, Thomas, may have predeceased his father; only two surviving sons, Benjamin Flye and Edmund, the executor, are named in Alexander's will of 1680. Joan Johnson, described as his 'loving wife', was left £100 in gold already in her keeping together with the goods she brought to their marriage and £10 per annum; also the room she then occupied if she pleased to live with executor, Edmund, her step-son. This arrangement was often used to provide living quarters for a widow when she was not left the bulk of the estate. The elderly Alexander and Joan were probably living with Edmund who was managing the business for them. Alexander could have been aged eighty at his death (he was admitted freeman in 1628 – fifty years earlier). Edmund, as eldest surviving son, would inherit the mercery business; younger son Benjamin was left £100. There was no mention of the Flye family properties in Alexander's will, though Joan had inherited a half share in her father, Saloman Flye's, property next to the guildhall on the death of her brother Robert. In 1669 Joan and Alexander Johnson demised this half share by a 7-year lease[23] to Joan's sister, Elizabeth Cooper, widow of alderman Robert Cooper who died in 1662.[24] 1669 produced several bonds for moneys lent between the Johnson and Cooper families including one of £140 between Elizabeth's eldest son, John Cooper, a goldsmith in London, and Alexander Johnson.[25]

Edmund Johnson's career in local office began before his father's death and followed the same path. He was made overseer of the poor in 1683 and soon achieved higher office, signing the churchwardens' accounts as mayor in 1687 and 1688.

Edmund died in 1688; his will reveals more family information. His wife had predeceased him; although the parish register entry reads 'Elizabeth, d. of Mr. Edmund', it was his wife Elizabeth Johnson whose burial was registered in 1687. She probably died of scrofula (a disease similar to tuberculosis) having been issued with a certificate for 'the King's evil' by the churchwardens in 1687.[26] Edmund mentions his brother Benjamin and his wife, both still living, and the children of his brothers Thomas and Alexander. Elizabeth Stevens, a married niece, was the

Signatures of Alexander Johnson and his two sons, Edmund and Benjamin. All three held the position of alderman of Woodstock.

daughter of Thomas, and there was a nephew, Alexander Johnson, whose father was not identified. Edmund seemed much attached to his late wife's family, the Palmers, leaving them money for rings and naming his father in law Palmer as executor. Edmund's 'three dear children' Edmund, Elizabeth and Grace, inherited equal parts of his estate after payment of legacies. Another son, Benjamin, baptised in 1683 seems not to have survived. All three children were under eight years of age but no guardians were appointed.[27] 'Mr. Edmund Johnson, alderman', was buried on 5th November 1688. His inventory, exhibited on 27th September 1689, had notable items such as £98 in his purse, 7 gold rings and 23 pairs of sheets. Shop goods, not itemised, were valued at £494. The total inventory value was £1006, reducing to £792 after payment of shop debts.[28]

Joan Johnson, Alexander's widow, died in 1695 outliving her stepson Edmund by several years. It was Benjamin, described as her natural son (i.e. blood related), who administered her estate; inventory value was £144 of which £100 was in debts 'hopeful of recovery'.[29]

Benjamin Flye Johnson, youngest son of Alexander and Joan, made an advantageous marriage to Grace, the daughter of another Woodstock mercer, Thomas Sparrow.

The Sparrow family

Thomas Sparrow, an incomer to the town, possibly from Leafield where he owned property, was resident by the early 1650's owning a shop in Market Street, now Bartholomew House, which had been John Bradshaw's. Soon seeking advancement he was appointed overseer to the poor in 1655, chamberlain in 1659 then alderman and

Signature of alderman Thomas Sparrow, mercer, father in law of Benjamin Johnson.

mayor by 1662, holding office several times until his death in 1678.[30] The goods described in his inventory are very similar in range to Bradshaw's suggesting uninterupted use of the house as a mercer's premises. Sparrow's stock included 50 dozen candles and tallow in the workshop; fine accessories in haberdashery were for sale alongside earthenwares, gunpowder, Bibles, brown paper and brandy. Sugar ('suggers') was valued at £22. Overall inventory valuations were modest and the total estate £666 with debts due of £308. The Sparrows had one surviving child, their daughter Grace, who received £400 in her father's will.[31]

The marriage of Benjamin Flye Johnson and Grace Sparrow, not entered in Woodstock registers, took place before 1690, the year Elizabeth Sparrow, Grace's mother, died leaving her daughter a further £200 and appointing Benjamin, her son in law, sole executor. Her inventory lists £230 hopeful debts in a total value of £314.[32] Benjamin took over Thomas Sparrow's business and shop on his marriage giving him control of a large proportion of the mercery trade within Woodstock.

Benjamin Flye Johnson probably stepping into his late brother's shoes, became alderman and mayor in the 1690s.[33] However the earlier 17th century system of influential families holding office by intermarriage disappeared after the restoration as local gentry began to take an interest in Woodstock affairs and joined the council. In the early 18th century Queen Anne granted the old royal park to John and Sarah Churchill, as duke and duchess of Marlborough. Their influence on the town was felt to a much greater degree than that of the monarchs on their occasional visits. The Marlboroughs brought an influx of professionals and craftsmen to the town both during and following the building of Blenheim Palace. This trade helped to make Benjamin Johnson one of the wealthiest residents.

Benjamin and Grace Johnson had no children to survive them. They raised Edmund Johnson's young family after his death in 1688. Edmund's daughter Grace married mercer, John Davis, Benjamin's apprentice.[34] The couple had three children, Benjamin, Edmund and Grace, baptised before John Davis's death in 1710. So Benjamin and Grace Johnson supported at least two of Edmund's children, Elizabeth, unmarried and

Grace Davis, a widow with three young children. Grace was not an economic burden on her uncle and aunt as John Davis had left property valued at over £1000 after payment of his considerable debts of £2300. The Davis's had a comfortable house with rooms named Blue and Red, chambers over hall and shop, kitchen, cellar and workroom. Linen included 20 pairs of sheets and 20 tablecloths. They had a small amount of silver. The main wealth was contained in the shop goods, valued at £2100 and an 800-year lease of tithes in Tysoe valued at £1000.[35]

Elizabeth Johnson, daughter of Edmund (d.1688) died unmarried in 1711. Her sister Grace Davis and uncle, Benjamin Johnson, administered her estate valued at £500 with debts owing of £450 thought hopeful of recovery.[36]

Grace Johnson (nee Sparrow) wife of Benjamin, died in 1714 aged 53. She was buried in Woodstock church; Benjamin provided a memorial stone, set into the floor near the south door.

Here lyeth the Body of Grace
The Wife of BENJAMIN
JOHNSON Alderman of this
Burrough Who Departed
this life the 3 day of April
Anno Dom 1714 Aged
53 years

Benjamin Johnson, now very wealthy, died in 1715. His will's first bequest was £50 to the town for schooling of five poor children of Woodstock freemen. A codicil provided a further £20 to buy blue coats for these children and £10 for 'a handsome branch candelabra for the church of Woodstock'. He left the residue of his estate to 'my niece Grace Davis, widow, now living with me'. Her three children by John Davis were left £400 each at age 21; Benjamin Davis, the eldest, also received a house and lands in Kidlington and the house and lease of the George Inn (now Marlborough Arms) in Woodstock. The Leafield estate, which Grace Sparrow brought to the marriage, was very properly left to John Sparrow, a member of her family, but with a proviso of loss of the bequest if he 'make any trouble at law' or claim other estate of the late Thomas Sparrow. A cousin, Alexander Johnson of London, is mentioned and inherited £200 and Alexander's brothers 'if they are alive' £10 apiece. So the younger Johnsons had not kept close ties with their Woodstock relatives. Benjamin's household goods were of modest value, his wealth lay in land and investments. His six-roomed house contained some pewter and silver but very ordinary furnishings. The item 'one tallow press and mould rods in the workhouse' suggests he was living at Thomas Sparrow's former residence, Bartholomew House. Debts owing to Benjamin were £1500 hopeful of recovery and £200 desperate bringing total inventory value to £1616.[37]

So in just five years Grace Davis lost her husband, her sister, and the aunt and uncle who had raised her. However, she was very wealthy and soon found another suitor in Edward Ryves, son of Woodstock town clerk, George Ryves. Edward and Grace married in 1715. The marriage united two powerful Woodstock families with forbears dating back to the late 16th century. No doubt helped by Grace's fortune, Edward Ryves became a wealthy property owner within the town and district.

The Ryves family

The Ryves can be traced back to Thomas Rawlins town clerk of Woodstock from 1598. Although granted the post for life, he retired in favour of his son in law, Edmund Hiorne, in 1607. Hiorne was the most noted town clerk of his time; much knowledge of 17th century Woodstock is due to his careful records. John Williams replaced him as town clerk for the commonwealth period. Reinstated from 1662, Hiorne resigned the following year in favour of George Ryves, husband of his granddaughter Anne Fleetwood. George was clerk until his death in 1677; the post returned briefly to the Williams family until the death of John Williams junior in 1681. That year George Ryves the younger, son of George and Anne (nee Fleetwood), took over and the post remained in the family for most of the next century. Edward Ryves, born in 1690, was the eldest surviving son of George and Margaret Ryves and his clerkship began in 1718 on the death of his father.

The family of Edward and Grace Ryves is recorded in the parish registers. They were married for over fifty years and had eight children. However they knew the pain of losing two of their sons as young men; Edward Ryves, their eldest son, died in September 1753 aged 36 and John, youngest son, died in November 1752, aged 25. Edward Ryves esq., died in 1767, and his widow Grace in 1774. The four are commemorated on a tablet in Woodstock church.

To the Memory of Edward Ryves, Grace his wife
and two of their sons, Edward and John
Edward Ryves Esq. departed this life April 14th 1767 aged 76 years
Grace Ryves died December 7th 1774 aged 88
Edward September 18th 1753 aged 36 John November 1752 aged 25

References

1   ORO MSS. Wills (Oxon), 106:15, 4/3/45, 4/4/17.
2   *WCA*, 75.
3   *WCA*, 119.
4   *WCBk*, 20.
5   WBM B78/2 *f 45v.*
6   *WCA*, 97.
7   ORO MSS. Wills (Oxon), 71/1/21
8   Churchwardens accounts 42.
9   WBM B81.
10 *WCA*, 206.
11 *WCA*, 234.
12 WBM Council minutes 1661 – 1670.
13 ORO MSS. Wills (Oxon), 71/4/1.
14 WBM, 78/2 and 3; *WCBk.*
15 ORO MSS. Wills (Oxon), 21/4/30.
16 WBM Indenture B 21/3/-.
17 WBM Deed of settlement B 13/2/7.
18 WBM Indenture B 21/3/- .
19 WBM B 78/3 *f 141.*
20 WBM Indenture B 13/1/2.
21 *VCH Oxon*, xii, 355.
22 ORO MSS. Wills (Oxon), 38/1/18.
23 WBM Indenture of lease B 13/1/2.
24 ORO MSS. Wills (Oxon), 13/4/12.
25 WBM Bond B 13/1/8.
26 It was thought that the king's touch could cure the disease.
27 By law children could choose their own guardian when aged seven. Edmund's brother Benjamin raised the three children.
28 ORO MSS. Wills (Oxon), 38/2/10.
29 ORO MSS. Wills (Oxon), 168/3/36.
30 *WCA*, 237.
31 ORO MSS. Wills (Oxon), 62/1/9.
32 ORO MSS. Wills (Oxon), 62/4/11.
33 WBM B96 Inhabitants' lists.
34 *VCH Oxon*, xii, 362.
35 ORO MSS. Wills (Oxon), 164/2/43.
36 ORO MSS. Wills (Oxon), 168/4/10.
37 ORO MSS. Wills (Oxon), 137/1/28.

Nash family of Old Woodstock

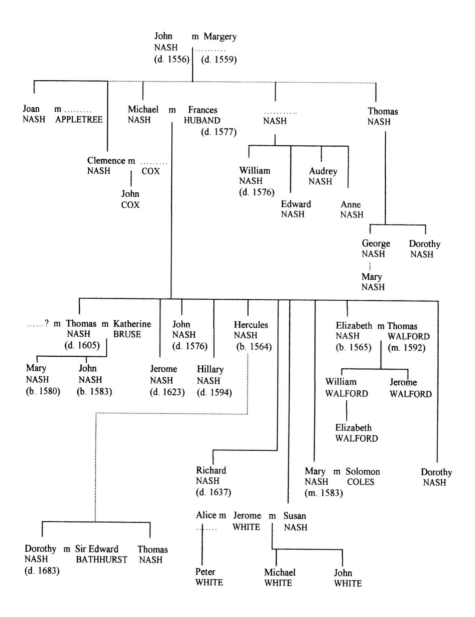

The Nash family of Old Woodstock

A memorial to John Nash in Bicester Church depicted his coat of arms: "Azure, on a chevron, between 3 birds erased argent, a pellet between 4 cross crosslets, sable, impaling quarterly of four; 1 Huband, 2 Danvers, 3 Burley, 4 Pury". Above the said arms he was described as 'Nash of Old Woodstock'.[1]

The Nashes lived in Old Woodstock for over fifty years occupying the most important house, Praunces Place (now Manor Farm). John Nash was perhaps the first family member to hold property in Old Woodstock though it is unclear if he was a resident. The house was leased from Balliol College; before 1530 they had acquired part of the house and land in the area from Thomas Harrope, Rector of Great Haseley, an ex-Fellow of the College.[2]

The wills of John Nash of Bicester (died 1556) and his widow, Margery (died 1559),[3] do not prove they were the parents of Michael Nash of Old Woodstock, but they seem the only candidates. They leased land and owned three houses in Bicester but were not exceptionally wealthy. Both wills named two daughters, Joan Appletree and Clemence Cox, as beneficiaries, but there is no mention of land or family in Old Woodstock. Nevertheless, John Nash of Bicester was stated to have been the father of Michael Nash who definitely lived in Praunces Place;[4] perhaps taking over his father's Old Woodstock leases when his parents retired to Bicester. Michael's family first occupied the east wing of the house belonging to Balliol.

The Nash family coat of arms.

In 1564 he purchased the west wing from William Seacole of Stanton Harcourt, and in the next decade carried out a programme of building and renovation work to the house.[5]

Michael Nash was a lawyer by profession, officiating as attorney at the Court of Common Pleas.[6] Training at Inns of Chancery, attorneys were regarded as lesser practitioners in the law and restricted to representing absent clients in the Courts.[7] To appear at the Court of Common Pleas Michael would have had to travel to London, as this Court always sat at Westminster. Occasionally cases heard by Woodstock portmoot court were referred to Common Pleas for a decision.

Traditionally Michael would have left his wife at home raising the children and overseeing the estate management.[8] When Sir Henry Lee was appointed Steward of Woodstock Park by Queen Elizabeth I, he reportedly found the existing tenants troublesome, especially the Gregorys of Hordley.[9] Michael Nash had similar problems. In 1568 he wrote to the Steward quoting some of the local customs and pointing out that only five parties had common rights at Old Woodstock Sarte, (a clearing south of Wootton Wood). He complained that non-commoners Raphe Pufford and William Horn of Wootton had allowed their cattle into the Sarte last winter causing much damage to the corn and given 'lowd words' when told of it.[10] Michael asked for Sir Henry's intervention in the dispute and in response may have been allowed to enclose the Old Woodstock portion of the field for his own use. These early enclosures by the gentry, though on a smaller scale than those of the 18th century which ended the open field system of farming, were nonetheless unpopular with smaller landholders, husbandmen and cottagers, who were denied their common rights. In the 1590's there was agricultural unrest in the Woodstock area when the price of corn rose and food shortages occurred following a series of bad harvests.[11] The enclosure practice was thought partly to blame.

Michael Nash married Frances Huband of Ippesley, Warwickshire.[12] They had ten children, some of whose baptisms appear in Wootton registers. Such large families were not uncommon among gentry at the time.[13] One reason was 'safety in numbers'; several children of a family could die in epidemics such as smallpox or plague and bigger families hopefully ensured some survivors to continue the family name and inherit the wealth. However, the Nash's seem to have been healthy enough, only the third son, John, who died in 1576, did not reach his majority.[14]

Perhaps Michael Nash was ill when he wrote his will in 1570.[15] Usually wills were made when the testator was thought near to death but Michael lived a further seven years. The will named all his children, six sons, Thomas, Jerome, John, Hillary, Hercules and Richard and four daughters, Dorothy, Mary, Susan and Elizabeth. He left each child 20 marks (£13 6s 8d) payable at 24 years of age or marriage. Thomas, as eldest son, received some personal property, his father's cloak, lute and a cornelian ring. Frances was requested to divide Michael's collection of books between their children. She received the income from his lands, reverting on her remarriage or death to Thomas and his heirs and to each of the other sons in order of age, or, if none survived, to each of the daughters and, lastly, to a nephew, William Nash. Frances was executrix and required to administer within six months or else lose the executorship to all her sons acting jointly, or if none survived, to all her daughters. If Frances renounced execution she received only 100 marks, her clothing, jewels and the best gelding.

The nephew mentioned was perhaps William Nash who died in 1574.[16] He was a young servant to George Whitton, comptroller of Woodstock Park, and left a will disposing of many interesting personal effects and clothing. He also named younger brothers and sisters, Edward, Audrey and Ann, and an uncle, Thomas Nash, who had two children, Dorothy and George. Since these families were contemporary with Michael Nash's, it is just possible that Michael, Thomas and William's father were three brothers, sons of John and Marjorie Nash.

Michael Nash died in 1577. One of the overseers of his will, described as William Babbington, esquire, bore the same name as the sheriff of Oxfordshire, Sir William Babbington, who died of a mysterious 'pestilence', thought to be a form of typhus, which overtook Oxford Assizes in July 1577.[17] The assize became known as the 'Black Assizes' as it was thought some 300 persons died in its aftermath. It is interesting to note that Michael Nash was buried in St.Mary Magdalene church in Woodstock on 17th August 1577.[18] As an attorney, could he have been one of the victims? His wife, Frances, had perhaps predeceased him, although her burial is not entered in the local registers. Thomas, eldest son, appeared as administrator in the probate clause of Michael's will, supporting that possibility. Frances was also buried in Woodstock church.[19]

The name of Thomas Nash, eldest son of Michael, does not appear often in local documents, but two children of a Thomas Nash were baptised at Wootton, Mary in 1580 and John in 1583. Also a Thomas Nash married Katherine Bruse of Hensington in 1602, perhaps a second marriage and probably he was the same Thomas Nash of Woodstock who died in 1605 and whose daughter Mary administered his estate in that year. Mary's guarantor to the bond was Thomas Norwood, head of a family of gentry from Hensington parish.[20]

Hillary Nash, third son of Michael and Frances, died in 1594. He was a city of London mercer and, although he died fairly young, had acquired considerable wealth in this trade. He may have spent his last days in Woodstock as John Taylford, parson of Wootton, witnessed his will.[21] Hillary requested burial in the church of New Woodstock and gave 40s each to the poor of Woodstock and Wootton. His specific bequests to his brothers and sisters were all in cash, £200 to Jerome, £100 to Hercules, £150 to Richard, £50 each at 21 years to nephews, Michael and John, sons of his sister Susan and her husband Jerome White of Woodstock, £50 to sister Elizabeth Woodford (als. Walford) and her children. The residue, perhaps including his stock in trade, went to Jerome Nash as executor after payment of £20 each to Hillary's partners Messrs. True and Heath. These generous bequests settled considerable wealth on the Nash family in Woodstock. It was partly due to Hillary's diligence and success that Jerome and his younger brothers enjoyed such a high standard of living in their later years.

Elizabeth Nash married Thomas Walford of Hensington in 1592;[22] there were at least two sons of the marriage, William and Jerome. The latter, described as a yeoman, appeared at a sessions court in Woodstock in April 1615 being bound over to keep the peace; he was dismissed at the next sessions. In January 1619 Walford was arrested by the sergeant at the behest of Richard Bently, two Woodstock residents Robert Banting and Robert Bignill refused to assist and Walford escaped via Bignill's house after injuring the sergeant.[23] William Walford's name appears in chamberlains' accounts of the late 1630's when he visited the town concerning Richard Nash's bequest. Ten years later Walford's heirs were still paying rent for Dovehouse Close in Old Woodstock, once leased to Jerome Nash.[24]

Hillary's will shows that Susan Nash married Jerome White a Woodstock resident from before 1588. From that year his name appears frequently in the portmoot court records where he appeared often as pledge and juror.[25] He was elected to the common council in January 1598.[26] A shoemaker by trade and also a licensed victualler he was appointed sergeant at mace in October 1617, which allowed him to act as a portmoot attorney. The office of sergeant was conferred for life but Jerome's tenure was very short; he died on 18th February 1618. Susan, his wife, had died earlier and Jerome's second wife was named Alice. Their son, Peter, was apprenticed to John Phillips, weaver, in 1619.[27] Susan's sons Michael and John, mentioned in Hillary's will, have not been traced.

Hercules Nash is mentioned occasionally in Woodstock documents of his time. The court book of 1588-95 lists several actions against him including one for assault and battery in 1591 brought by John Phillips of the borough. No details are recorded but Phillips was awarded damages. Another notable Woodstock resident, William Metcalf, woollendraper, sued for trespass in 1593.[28] In the same court in 1609 a plaintiff is named as Henry Nasshe but this may be a copyists error. The case is interesting in that John Woodruffe of Old Woodstock, sued for debt by Nasshe, used wager of law to prove his case and came to court with six 'hands' to support his good name. These men were of the top rank in Woodstock society (John Glover, Thomas Williams, Thomas Screevin, Ralph Durbridge, Edward Long and Francis Garter) and not surprisingly Woodruffe was acquitted.[29] There are no probate documents for Hercules Nash and his burial date is not traced.

It was Jerome Nash and his youngest brother, Richard Nash, whose names appeared on all leases and other deeds concerning their Old Woodstock properties. Both followed academic careers at Oxford; Jerome became Fellow of St. John's College in 1573, obtaining a BA in 1577 and an MA in 1580 from Brasenose. In 1581 he took a BCL degree to practise in common law like his father.[30] Richard obtained a BA from Magdalen Hall in 1588.[31] Jerome used his legal knowledge in negotiations with Balliol and may have acted as their local land agent.[32] In 1589 he leased the Old Woodstock properties for a term of three lives, offering the College, among other things, plate worth £3 6s 8d should he wish to re-negotiate.[33] A clause allowed the college use of some rooms in Praunces Place for the masters and 12 scholars at times when plague threatened Oxford. Accordingly, in 1604 several college members arrived in Woodstock. Unfortunately King James I was also sheltering at Woodstock that summer and they were required to keep to the house and adjoining fields and not allowed to enter the town or present themselves at Court for fear of infecting the king.[34]

Jerome also leased property from Woodstock corporation including Dovehouse Close in Old Woodstock, situated between the park wall and highway. He demolished the dovehouse itself in 1608.[35] He owned other Woodstock properties at different times. In 1611 these included a house (or possibly an inn) known as 'the sign of the Talbot' in High or Park Gate street (now Park Street) and three cottages to the east of the lane to Hoggerill hill (now Hoggrove).[36] Additionally he was renting Michael Pulgoe's house and a house by the bridge footway (at Browns Lane).[37] Jerome also served as executor or overseer to some Woodstock wills of the early 17th century including that of alderman Thomas Bradshaw, wealthy innkeeper and landlord of The Bull in New Woodstock.[38] The inn was

Signature of Jerome Nash (d.1623).

favoured by the nobility visiting Woodstock manor; a convenient place for the Nashes to meet with their own social class.

Jerome appeared in estate documents of Sir Henry Lee of Ditchley and possibly helped Sir Henry in a legal ploy to sell his entailed lands at Quarrendon, Bucks. Richard Nash, holding a post in the Lee household, witnessed several of these indentures. He was also witness and beneficiary to Sir Henry's will. Both brothers took part in Sir Henry's state funeral procession in 1611; 'Mr.Jherome Nashe' walked ahead of the coffin and Mr Richard Nash, as honorary bearer, beside it.[39]

In 1615 Jerome and Richard, acting jointly, sold the west wing of Praunces Place to Balliol College together with nearly 100 acres of family estate in the area and 50 acres of Old Woodstock Sarte,[40] which they now owned, probably as a result of further enclosing. The price they obtained was £700.[41] By comparison a lease of one acre of pasture in Old Woodstock was sold in the same year for £2.10s.[42]

Jerome Nash died on 20th September 1623. In his will dated 8th September he expressed a wish to be buried in Woodstock church with his parents and other kindred. He left bequests to the poor of Woodstock and the seven parishes of the manor, £20 to a godson, Francis Nash Gregory, and his books, except those on Common Law, to kinsman Francis Chenell. The residue went to his 'loving brother' Richard. Perhaps prompted by the beneficiaries, he added a codicil on 19th September recalling that he gave the bed he lay on, and its bedding, to Francis Gregory and his wife Anne. He also gave them room and board in his house for a year following his death. He remembered too his old servant, Guy Beckley, and gave him a dwelling house for life for a noble (6s 8d) a year.[43] The Gregorys were of the Hordley family and Jerome's godson, Francis Nash Gregory, became Master of the Free School in Woodstock in 1660.[44]

Executor Richard Nash drew up a detailed inventory of every item in the house and adjoining farmstead, revealing the high standard of living enjoyed and efficient farm management. The inventory lists contents of each room with additional lists of silverware, pewter, linen and Jerome's wearing apparel. The latter suggests that he appeared a sombre figure since all his clothes, where identified by colour, were black. They included gowns, cloak, suits, jerkins, shirts and stockings in a variety of materials, serge, velvet, bayes, wool, silk, bustian and 'Philip & Cheyney'.[45] Gloves

An 1821 Buckler drawing of Manor Farm in Old Woodstock, the family home of the Nashes. The frontage shows some features of the work carried out by Michael Nash in the 16th century.

included a splendid pair laced with silk and gold. There were shoes of white and spanish leather and, for indoors, some lined slippers. He liked fine accessories, satin, lace, blackwork handkerchief, gold and silk nightcap and black silk garters.

The comfortable parlour contained leather chairs, hanging pictures, map and chess set. Downstairs were kitchen, larder, hall, dairy and brew-house. There were nine bedchambers, Mr. Jerome's contained bed and bedding, close stool and fireplace. Two brothers retained rooms in the house; that of Mr. Hercules only sparsely furnished, but Mr. Richard's included new feather bed, desk and chairs. Another chamber, grandly named 'the painted chamber' had wall hangings, and was perhaps for important guests. These would have been well entertained; among silver and pewter for the table were great chargers for meat, dishes for salad, broth and fruit, with pastry and pie plates. In a buttery were hogsheads and drink barrels. The dairy had cheese press, butter churns and milk pans. Bacon hung in a loft.

Outdoors the inventory listed equipment for a productive farm. Livestock included a few cows and pigs, a team of horses and nearly 200 sheep and lambs valued at £40. The area was well suited to sheep rearing and the wool trade, though past its medieval peak, still flourished. Woodstock was a staple town for wool and numbered woolmen among its inhabitants. Farm implements included ploughs, harrows, carts and hand tools. Cereals, pulses and hops were grown, all safely harvested when the inventory was compiled in October 1623. These crops were valued at £113; perhaps some would be needed to pay the rent; Oxford colleges had introduced corn rents in the late 16th century.[46]

Among leases valued were Balliol and Magdalen Colleges'; Balliol's worth only 1 shilling, but Magdalen's valued at £18. The ancient pastures called St. John's Croft and Barley Croft were probably leased from the College.[47] The total inventory value was £354. The first quarter of the 17th century saw the demise of several New Woodstock tradesmen of similar wealth to Jerome, but in Old Woodstock there was nobody to compare. One of the better-off inhabitants, Richard Banting, a tanner who died in 1628, left only £18. [48]

Richard Nash, Michael's youngest son, held a post in Sir Henry Lee's household at Ditchley. It was quite usual for minor gentry such as Nashes to act as servants to nobility. Richard witnessed Sir Henry's will and attested at an inquiry regarding the estate's distribution. Whilst at Ditchley, he acquired some land at nearby Stonesfield; in 1607 owning a messuage and 15 acres in the common fields there[49] but seemingly he returned to live in his brother's house for the later years of their lives. Richard made his will in 1635.[50] He requested burial in Woodstock Church and, like Jerome, left bequests to the poor of Woodstock manor's seven parishes. Such wide-ranging bequests were unusual; most testators left money to the poor of their own parish and perhaps the parish of their birth, but in the case of the Nash brothers, the family's status in the neighbourhood may have required greater generosity.

Richard Nash left £20 each to three nieces, Anne Jeffrey, Frances Richardson, and Elizabeth Hynoune. The surnames give no clues to their parentage, but, helpfully, Anne is identified as married to John Jeffrey of Old Woodstock, and probably Thomas (baptised 1632) and Anne (baptised 1634) were her children. Richard's lands in New and Old Woodstock and Wootton were left to his nephew, William Walford, son of Elizabeth Walford (nee Nash).[51] If William died childless these lands reverted to Anne Jeffrey. A marginal note states that Elizabeth Walford, William's daughter, administered Richard's estate in 1646 after her father's death. Richard left a generous bequest to the borough of New Woodstock; £80 for interest-free loans to 'honest towneborne, decayed tradesmen and women' and other similarly placed residents. He also left £20 for purchase of land to finance an annual sermon in his name.

After Richard's death in 1637, the family name disappeared from the area. Just one further entry in the registers records the marriage of Charity Nash to Robert House at Wootton in 1639. However in the female line, Frances Richardson lived in Old Woodstock until her death in 1663,[52] her second marriage was to George Daysey. Her son, Francis, died in Woodstock ten years later.[53] Ann Jeffery's son, Thomas, remained in Old Woodstock also; nearing the end of his life in 1713 he made a deed of gift of his close there to his daughter, Elizabeth Pinner of London.[54]

Much later in the 17th century Dame Dorothy Bathhurst, widow, second wife of Sir Edward Bathhurst of Lechlade, came to live in Woodstock. She drew her will in 1683 being 'of some little distemper of body at this present'.[55] There were bequests of cash to Sir Edward's sons and daughters and clothing and personal belongings to her many friends. She was clearly a fashionable lady with bequests including a black satin mantle, petticoats of black gauze and flowered satin, a muff and an 'allamode' scarf. A £30 legacy to her brother Thomas Nash identifies her birth surname. At her burial in Spelsbury church in 1683 the churchwardens noted 'she was the daughter of Mr. Nash of Woodstock'.[56] This raises the question of her parentage. She could not be the Dorothy Nash, daughter of Michael, mentioned in his will of 1570 nor the cousin of William Nash (d.1576). Thomas Nash, eldest son of Michael, had two known children whose baptisms are registered in the 1580's. Jerome, Hillary and Richard mention no spouses or children in their wills, suggesting they may all have remained bachelors. Hercules Nash was baptised in 1564 and was probably living until about 1610; he may have had a wife and children from whom Dorothy was descended. Likewise he could have been father of some of Richard Nash's three nieces mentioned in 1637.

Other probable relatives include Thomas Nash who married Elizabeth Hall, granddaughter of William Shakespeare.[57] Another Nash family lived in Walberton, Sussex from Restoration to early 19th century. A stone in St. Mary's church, Walberton, commemorated Thomas Nash of Walberton, son of Thomas Nash of Cambridge (died 1663). The coat of arms proves the family link as it appeared on a chalice presented to Walberton church in 1799. The same arms belonged to a Nash who, in 1772, became Lord Mayor of London.[58]

Previously published in *OLHA Journal* Vol 3 no 7, Autumn 1991.

References

1   Marshall, 166.
2   Jones, 47.
3   ORO MSS. Wills (Oxon), 181:34; 183:163.
4   Marshall, 166.
5   *VCH Oxon,* xii, 425/6.
6   Aston, 571.
7   Information – Hon. Soc. Inner Temple.
8   Houlbrooke.
9   Chambers, 93.
10   ORO, Lee V/1.
11   Chambers, 165.
12   Marshall, 166.
13   Houlbrooke.
14   Wootton burial register.
15   ORO MSS. Wills (Oxon), 186:32.
16   ORO MSS. Wills (Oxon), 185:249.
17   Norwood, 13.
18   Wootton burial register.
19   See will of Jerome Nash (d.1623).
20   ORO MSS. Wills (Oxon), 171/1/6.
21   PRO PROB 11/84.
22   Wootton marriage register.
23   WBM B78/3 *ff 37, 148.*
24   *WCA,* 228.
25   *WCBk.*
26   WBM B82.
27   WBM B78/3 *f 119, 160.*
28   *WCBk,* 38, 73.
29   WBM B78/2 *f 70.*
30   OHS Register of Univ.Oxford 11, iii, 68.
31   ditto 1, iii, 151.
32   Information Dr. J. Jones, Balliol College Archives.
33   Information Brig. Jackson, former bursar – an alms plate in Balliol College chapel is inscribed *Jerome Nashe of Woodstock gave this plate to Balliol College, Boswell B.D. (sometime fellow of the college) had it made.*
34   Jones, 66.
35   *WCA,* 34.
36   WBM (Flye family deed) B 13/2/7.
37   *WCA,* 41.
38   ORO MSS. Wills (Oxon), 4/3/17.
39   Chambers, 299.
40   Sarte – a clearing in a wood or forest to provide grazing or arable use.
41   Aston, 563.
42   ORO Deeds of Spittle house close, Woodstock.
43   ORO MSS. Wills (Oxon), 47/2/40.

44 *VCH Oxon,* xii, 417.
45 'Philip & Cheyney' – a kind of worsted or woollen stuff of common quality (OED).
46 Aston p.564.
47 *VCH Oxon,* xii, 427.
48 ORO MSS. Wills (Oxon), 5/2/23.
49 Howard Gray, 510.
50 PRO PROB 11/174.
51 Wootton marriage registers.
52 ORO MSS. Wills (Oxon), 107:128, 18/3/20.
53 ORO MSS. Wills (Oxon), 299/7/57.
54 ORO Deeds of Spittle house close, Woodstock
55 PRO PROB 11/375.38.
56 Corbett,125.
57 Chambers, 234.
58 Huxford, 286.

Whitton family of Woodstock Park

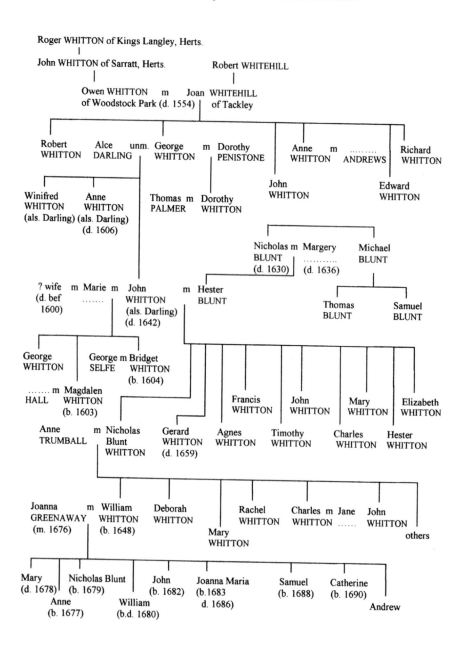

The Whitton family of Woodstock Park

The Whitton family coat of arms is described as *"Argent, on a chevron Sable five bezants a bordure engrailed of the second"*.

The family was established in Woodstock from the early 16th century. Its origins can be traced back to Roger Whitton of Kings Langley, Hertfordshire, who had two sons, John and Richard. John was probably the same John Whitton of Sarratt, Hertfordshire, who had three sons Edmund, Roger and Owen. It was the youngest son, Owen Whitton who settled in Woodstock.[1] In about 1520 he married Joan Whitehill, daughter of Robert Whitehill of Tackley, Oxfordshire, who held the post of comptroller of Woodstock Park under King Henry VII.[2] In 1523 Whitehill gave up the post and was succeeded by his son-in-law.

Owen inherited the Whitehill family estates in Tackley and eventually estates in Buckinghamshire also passed to the Whittons.[3] In 1543 he purchased the manor of Gosford near Kidlington, Oxon, but continued to live in the Woodstock area and became active in town affairs; he was elected mayor in 1551 and 1554.[4]

Due to the early date, Owen's Woodstock activities are not well documented and it is his will, signed on 20th April 1554, which gives a first insight into his family.[5] There were five sons, Robert, George, Richard, John and Edward. Richard was joint executor with his mother, Joan Whitton. A married daughter, Anne Andrews, was left £10 from the sale of sheep and cattle. Owen's wearing apparel, money and livestock were divided fairly between the five sons. Their mother received all household goods together with her 'rayment', jewels and £40 already in her custody. The estates Owen had acquired were not mentioned and may have been dealt with separately under laws of inheritance. Sir Leonard Chamberlain, Thomas Alruyh esquire and John Gelyman, parson of Hanborough, Oxon, were appointed overseers. The will was proved on

17th April 1555 with an inventory value of £104.

Owen's daughter Anne possibly married John or Edmund, sons of Richard Andrews of Woodstock (d.1554).[6] Andrews was a crown agent and with Sir Leonard Chamberlain, dealt with distribution of lands in the Woodstock area following Henry VIII's dissolution of the monasteries.[7] These family links were profitable in acquisition of the Whitton estates.

The most notable member of the Whitton family was George, second son of Owen Whitton. Robert, eldest son named in Owen's will, may have died as it was George who took over the family estates. George was born in Woodstock in about 1523; he attested to being 47 years of age at a church court in Oxford in 1570.[8] He succeeded to the post of comptroller on his father's death in 1554. Another quaintly named post held with controllership of the park was keeper of hares and woodwardship of Spelsbury manor. In 1556 George married Dorothy Penistone at Spelsbury;[9] she was the daughter of Thomas Penistone of Deane, Oxon, a kinsman to Sir Henry Lee.[10] The same year George sold his manor of Gosford later purchasing Hensington manor in Bladon parish.

During his fifty years as comptroller, George was active in all aspects of the town and manor; he became a JP and represented Woodstock in parliament from 1572.[11] He also became freeman and common councillor and served a term as mayor in 1571. However, with his turbulent character and outspokenness he caused much trouble within the town.

Around 1572 the post of Lieutenant or Steward of the manor of Woodstock and Master of the Game passed from the Chamberlain family, who had held stewardship since the time of Henry VII, to Sir Henry Lee. A nobleman and Champion of Elizabeth I, Lee held several offices during her reign, including Master of the Leash and Master of the Armoury at the tower of London. He spent his earlier years assisting in military campaigns and travelling in Europe.

The non-resident Chamberlain family was not diligent in its stewardship of the manor allowing extra responsibilities and opportunities to the Whittons. However, when Sir Henry Lee took over as steward, a senior post to comptroller, he took an active interest in local land, acquiring much extra pasture and enclosing large areas for his own use. As some of the land was in use by the Whittons controversies arose concerning ownership and land management. The post of steward held many privileges including entitlement to keep livestock and use of several properties within the park. Lee soon increased his stocks of sheep and took more land to increase the number of deer. The steward was required to maintain a stock of two thousand deer and for this Lee was allowed to increase the size of the park but in so doing he upset local tenants who lost their rights to common grazing. Sir Henry also sought leases of extra meadowland, formerly used by the Whitton family as tenants, which held privileges from the crown. After many disagreements Sir Henry tried to remove George Whitton from his post and eventually brought a court action citing the comptroller's alleged wrongdoings; Whitton lost the case and was imprisoned in the Marshalsea from December 1580 until June 1581.

About the same time, in 1580, a dispute arose concerning ownership of land in Hensington; the mayor and corporation of Woodstock claimed it as ancient estate of the borough but George Whitton declared it to be part of his manor of Hensington. He enclosed an area known as Sterting Grove and installed his men to keep possession. Matters deteriorated until an altercation in the street with William Skelton, then mayor of the borough, and in September 1581 culminated in a document being signed by all common council members whereby George was removed from office as alderman and disfranchised for disobedience to the mayor.[12] Some legal actions resulted from the dispute including one heard in court of Star Chamber whereby Whitton demanded fee farm rents due to the crown but the town claimed these had always been paid to the Lieutenant. Basically these quarrels were about which faction, townsfolk or gentry, should have control of the council. Whitton declared it was 'to the utter decay of the poor' that the town was in the hands of victuallers who were intent on keeping control of licensing for their own benefit.[13] The point was well made; late 16th and early 17th century aldermen were predominantly innholders. However, it was thought that Whitton had wished to establish himself as mayor for life.

The latter years of George Whitton's life seem less turbulent. He never rejoined the council but in late 1580's was still sitting as JP and in 1598 was among those who ousted town clerk, Edulph Dingley.[14] In 1596 rioting occurred in Woodstock and area due to a series of bad harvests; enclosures by Whitton, Sir Henry Lee and other local gentry were blamed.[15] In 1600 George retired as comptroller; Sir Henry wished George's nephew, Henry Whitton, to succeed to the post. He wrote to Sir Robert Cecil in support of Henry and told Cecil 'an ancient uncle of (Henry) has now held (the office) some fifty years'.[16]

George Whitton died in 1606; during his lifetime he had amassed a great deal of land and other property in the area and this was carefully distributed in his will of January 1606.[17] The will contains details of his family; wife, Dorothy, was still living but described as 'in weak estate and imperfection'. The couple had land held in jointure since their marriage so that the profits would be used for Dorothy's maintenance if she outlived George. There was one daughter of the marriage, also named Dorothy, she married Thomas Parker of Spernham, Warwickshire and was with child in 1606. The Parkers' legacy was a lease of Wytells manor in Olney, Bucks, paying £40 yearly to John Whitton.

George also had three base born children by his servant Alice Darling and his only son was usually known as John Whitton als. Darling. John's legacy was the manor of Hensington and all other lands in the parishes of Shipton-upon-Cherwell and Bladon, Oxon. If John prevented the lease at Olney being taken by Thomas and Dorothy Parker they were to inherit George's house in Hensington in lieu. George's two base daughters, Winifred and Anne, were left specific items of table silver and three hundred pounds each. Out of this six hundred pounds five hundred was owed to George on bond by Sir Henry Lee and one hundred by John Whitton. There must be some doubt whether the two girls received their legacies as both Sir Henry and John Whitton seemed habitually short of cash. Alice Darling was well provided for with fifty pounds and living accommodation in the malthouse as well as rents of three Woodstock houses for her lifetime. George's brothers John and Richard Whitton were forgiven their debts and each manservant received a year's wages and every maidservant five shillings. Nephew Henry Whitton received George's mansion house in Woodstock for himself and his heirs forever. This house is identified as standing on a large plot east of Park Lane, now 24 to 34 High Street.[18] Overseers were Sir William Spencer of Yarnton, Sir Laurence Tanfield, borough recorder, and John Snow, MA, of Oxford University.

Later that year George added a codicil as his daughter Anne had since died and directed her legacy to be divided between the son and daughters of John Whitton. Grandson George received one hundred pounds at age 21 and granddaughters Bridget and Magdalen fifty pounds each on their marriages. John Whitton proved the will in December 1606.

Considering his quarrelsome nature with outsiders George Whitton's will reveals him to have been a kind and honest family man. His wealth was fairly distributed according to the customs of the day; he made no attempt to conceal his illegitimate children and dealt respectfully with their mother, Alice Darling. Clearly proud of his family's service to the crown he left instructions and money for a memorial stone to himself, his father and grandfather noting their lengthy term as comptrollers from the time of King Henry VII. This kindlier side of his nature was apparently also shown in his dealings with the young princess Elizabeth during her detention in the gatehouse at Woodstock manor in 1553/4 in the reign of her sister Mary Tudor.[19]

Throughout his will George Whitton referred to his son John and 'Marie his nowe wife', a phrase which usually indicates there was a previous wife and, if that is the case, then John Whitton married three times. There is no record of burial for Marie or her possible predecessor but soon after his father's death John married Hester Blunt. She was the daughter and only child of Nicholas Blunt who in his 1630 will described himself as 'citizen and innholder of London now inhabiting in Woodstock'.[20] In a complex and lengthy will Nicholas left Margery his wife his manor of Shurdington ('Sherdington') in the county and city of Gloucester. Margery to pay £40 annually to Hester for life and £15 half yearly to Nicholas Blunt Whitton, Hester's eldest son, until he was 21. On Margery's death the manor reverted to Nicholas Blunt Whitton and his heirs and, if he died childless, to each of Hester's sons and daughters in turn. The children are named as Francis, Agnes, Elizabeth, Gerard, John, Timothy and Mary. (Gerard's will of 1658 also names siblings Charles and Hester).

One unusual clause in the will charged Margery with careful and frugal management and preservation of trees upon the Shurdington estate except six acres of coppice to be used at her will and pleasure. Trustees were appointed to manage the estate if Margery died before Nicholas reached 21 and they also were barred from felling trees to provide arable land. It is impossible to judge whether Blunt was opposed to woodland clearance from an aesthetic or conservation point of view or intended to preserve the valuable timber.

Blunt's will reveals the extent of his wealth and therefore John Whitton's advantageous marriage to Hester Blunt. In 1630 John owed his father in law One thousand two hundred pounds; six hundred repayable that year on the Feast of St. James. Margery, as executor would pay the total 'if it can be gotten' to Hester's children; one hundred pounds each to Francis, Gerard, John, Timothy, Agnes and Elizabeth with another six hundred pounds divided between the four boys; all for investment until the children came of age. Son-in-law John Whitton received a piece of gold, valued at ten shillings, as a token of remembrance. Francis Whitton proved the will in August 1656, it had lain unadministered by Margery Blunt who died in 1636. Hester Whitton also renounced administration.

The Woodstock corporation by custom presented a cake and a sugar loaf every Christmas to the High Steward of the borough.[21] Sir Henry Lee was Steward in the early 17th century and following his death in 1611 the post went to Sir Thomas Spencer. From 1617 the same Christmas gift also went to Sir Gerard Fleetwood, Woodstock's member of parliament from 1625.[22] The Fleetwoods lived in one of the park lodges[23] and held some responsibilities in management of the manor; park keeper William Todman who died in 1624 claimed to be owed wages for keeping of the red deer since Sir Gerard's coming.[24] Also in 1625 Sir Gerard was made official keeper of the manor house and in this he was succeeded in 1637 by his son, Sir William, who claimed the office of Ranger by 1649. Although the Fleetwoods' authority gradually increased, it appears that John and Nicholas Whitton were on amicable terms with them with no evidence of disagreements such as happened between George Whitton and Sir Henry Lee; perhaps the Fleetwoods left actual land management to the experienced Whittons.

During the early years of the 17th century John Whitton als. Darling was evidently in favour with Charles, Prince of Wales, who granted him the next presentation to the living of the ecclesiastical parish of Bladon with Woodstock.[25] In 1621, on the retirement of rector Edward Evans,

Signatures of John and Hester Whitton. John's two signatures differ illustrating the practise of official (court) and non-official (secretary) handwriting in use at the time.

Thomas Browne, son of the late Woodstock alderman of the same name, was awarded the post by John Whitton. On becoming king in 1625 Charles I granted John and his son and heir, Nicholas Blunt Whitton, use of the comptroller's lodgings in the royal manor house at Woodstock, together with certain rights of wood and hay from the park.[26] This grant may have restored some of the privileges taken away by Sir Henry Lee in the previous century.

John Whitton did not follow his father's example of involvement in Woodstock borough affairs and his name is not included on lists of freemen and inhabitants. However, several of his property transactions were noted in the portmoot court books; some can be identified as property previously owned by George Whitton.[27] In 1610 Henry Whitton quitclaimed his mansion house to John Whitton[28] and in 1626 Nicholas Blunt, Hester's father, took up residence in a 'great house' formerly owned by Edmund Hiorne.[29]

John was not a frequent user of the portmoot court but in 1615 he was pursued for a debt of £89 on loan from widow Anne Leake and after her death by her executor Robert Abbot, bishop of Salisbury. The action was referred to King's Bench court at Westminster, but this debt was eventually satisfied.[30] John Whitton was borrowing money throughout his life and of course he had twelve children to bring up, but he appears unprincipled in money matters generally, for instance he paid none of his rents due to the town for ten years up to 1625.[31]

Alice Darling, George Whitton's servant and mother of his three base-born children died in 1629. She left personal and household items to her granddaughters, Bridget and Magdalen Whitton. Grandson George was not mentioned and may have died by that date. [32]

John Whitton wrote his will on mid-summer day in 1642. His two eldest daughters are named as Magdalen Hall and Bridget Self. Magdalen's husband has not been traced but Bridget married George Selfe, an Oxford MA ordained in 1629 and curate of Woodstock from 1632-41.[33] John's only legacies were rings valued five shillings to his son Francis and daughters Magdalen and Bridget. Son Nicholas received a bow and a gun and the tithe of Woodstock park which was mortgaged to him for £100. Hester and Nicholas were executors and trusted to dispose of John's estate for the good of his unmarried children. The will was proved on 8th July 1643.[34]

From 1628 John Whitton and his eldest son Nicholas Blunt Whitton were joint Comptrollers of Works and Surveyors of the Forests for Woodstock manor, an arrangement probably continuing until John's death in 1642.[35] Due to events in the developing civil war the last months of John's life must have been uncomfortable. The manor was a royalist stronghold and well placed for lodging of officers supporting the King's Oxford headquarters. However this led to large numbers of troops being billeted within the town and surrounding area from time to time; normal management of the park must have been impossible; an arduous task for Nicholas, taking over on his father's death. The royal family stayed during any outbreak of plague in Oxford and still used the park for hunting. The king was at Woodstock in June 1644 prior to his famous overnight flight from Oxford and parliamentary forces arrived shortly afterwards to evict the small royalist garrison. From September 1644 the manor changed hands several times and a blockade began in 1646.[36] In April of that year the Woodstock garrison surrendered and this action precipitated the King's final exit from Oxford.

The Whitton's loyalties would have been to the king but it is not recorded how they coped with the constant changes in the war years. It was probably Nicholas Whitton's brother John who took arms for the king during the war and petitioned in 1661 for expenses incurred.[37]

By the end of hositilites the manor, often in poor repair, was in a ruinous state. As late as 1664 diarist John Evelyn wrote: 'October 18th At Oxford. . .Went thro' Woodstock, where we beheld the destruction of that royal seate and park by ye late rebels …'. [38]

Nicholas Blunt Whitton married Anne Trumball of Easthampstead, Berks, in 1639[39] and during the civil war years the couple were bringing up the eldest of their large family of five sons and eight daughters. Wootton baptism registers list Elizabeth in 1642 and Debra in 1644, both baptised in the King's chapel at Woodstock manor, William was baptised in 1648 and Martha in 1650. Other Whitton baptisms are registered in Woodstock and Wootton in the mid 17th century, these were children of Nicholas' brothers, John and Charles, who remained in the area during the civil war. Two marriages of Nicholas and Anne's children are registered at Wootton; Jonathan in 1670 and Elizabeth in 1663; she married Lawrence Gwinnett, probably a son of George Gwynnett of Bagworth, Glos, overseer of Nicholas Blunt's will.

Gerard Whitton, third son of John and Hester, was also resident in Woodstock park when he died in 1659. His simple, nuncupative, will left his goods, chattels and all debts due to him to his brother and sister, Charles and Hester Whitton, youngest of John and Hester's children and probably unmarried in 1659. Gerrard did not appear to leave a wife or children. He was a favourite with Woodstock ladies, the witnesses to his will were Ann Hiorne, Elizabeth Cooper, Anne Godfrey, Joan Bath and Priscilla Painter. John Williams, Woodstock's town clerk, was sole executor and Gyles Franklin, barber surgeon, the only male witness.[40]

In 1652 Lt. Col. Charles Fleetwood, son in law of Cromwell, purchased the dilapidated manor. Although his brother, Sir William, was a royalist, Charles Fleetwood was an ardent parliamentarian and by 1655 commanded seven counties, including Oxfordshire. He was member of parliament for Woodstock from 1654.[41] As the Fleetwood family's authority increased the post of comptroller became less important and later generations of the Whitton family had less involvement in management of the park. By 1649 Nicholas Blunt Whitton held the post of keeper in addition to comptroller.[42] In the time of his son William Whitton the post may have been little more than farmer/gamekeeper.

Nicholas Blunt Whitton died in 1680. His will is short considering the number of his children and surprisingly he left his manor of Shurdington

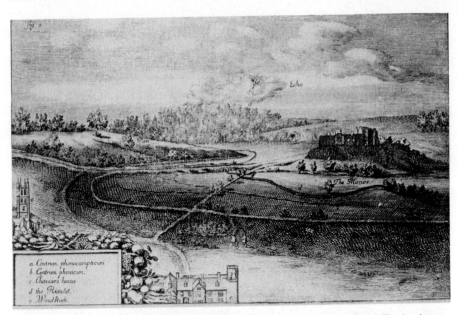

Dr. Plot's well known view of Woodstock manor house and surrounding parkland. The landscape would have looked similar throughout the Whitton family's tenure. The causeway to Woodstock provided access over the marshy ground of the Glyme valley.

jointly to three daughters, Deborah, Mary and Rachel and their heirs. Apparently none of the three sisters had children at that date and if any of them died without issue that share went to John, their youngest brother. Daughter Mary received the residue of the estate after payment of debts. Eldest son Charles Whitton, Jane his wife and grandson Nicholas Blunt Whitton are the only other family mentioned. Thomas Rowney of Oxford and George Gwynnet of Sherington, Glos, were executors. Nicholas was buried in Black Bourton, Oxon[43] where he spent his retirement years at the home of his son Charles.[44]

In 1676 William Whitton married Joanna Greenaway,[45] daughter of John Greenaway, manciple[46] to New College, Oxford. The couple had nine children, Mary (d.1678), Anne (b.1677), Nicholas Blunt (b.1679), William (b.d.1680), John (b.1682 d.1695), Joanna Maria (b.1683 d.1686), Samuel (b.1688), Catherine (b.1690) and Andrew (registration not found). The children's baptisms were registered mainly in Combe parish, the family apparently living in Combe lodge at that time.

William (born 1648), second son of Nicholas, was the final Whitton to hold the post of comptroller. The last decade of the Whittons' involvement with park and manor should have been pleasant enough. William grew arable crops as well as managing parkland and supplying browsing for deer raised within the walls.[47] He would have arranged some replanting to cover neglect during the civil war years and their aftermath. Following the restoration the park never gained popularity with the later Stuarts. In 1684 however, racecourses were laid down within the boundary and horse racing and foot racing became popular pastimes for the gentry.[48]

In 1705 Queen Anne granted the park and manor to John Churchill, Duke of Marlborough, in appreciation of his victories in the war of Spanish Succession. Samuel Travers, surveyor general of crown lands was ordered to clear the park of 'encumbrances'. Clearly the Whittons were regarded as an 'encumbrance' and with keepers and other park lodge residents were removed without ceremony. Lord Baltimore, last steward and ranger of the park, received around £7000 compensation and keepers were paid £900 apiece. William would have been similarly compensated but his exact payment is not recorded; in addition he sold his tithes of the park to the incoming Duke of Marlborough.[49] However, the suddenness of the operation would have fallen hard on the Whitton family. William was said to have left with some bad grace. Surveyor Travers wrote to the Marlboroughs in July 1705 saying 'with much ado I got out Whitton on Wednesday last and so the park is clear'.[50] Surely William can be forgiven for feeling some bitterness; he could trace his family's service to the royal manor for six generations and through the reigns of eleven monarchs.

References

1   Shipp J. correspondence with College of Arms, London. July 1992.
2   *VCH Oxon*, xii, 440.
3   *VCH Bucks*, iv, 436.
4   Marshall, (list of mayors).
5   ORO MSS. Wills (Oxon), 180:251.
6   PRO PROB 11/37.134.
7   Taylor RF, *Debts and credits in the Woodstock community 1530 – 1700* (unpublished).
8   ORO MSS. Oxf.diocesan papers *c21, f, 26v, 27, 27v.*
9   Spelsbury marriage registers.
10 Chambers, 95.
11 *VCH Oxon*, xii, 400.
12 Ballard, Ch. iv, *Troublous Times.*
13 Chambers, 82 – 101.
14 *VCH Oxon*, xii, 374.
15 Walter J., *The Oxfordshire Rising,* Past & Present, (1988).
16 Chambers, 103.
17 PRO PROB. 11/108.
18 *VCH Oxon*, xii, 355.
19 Chambers, 103.

20 PRO PROB 11/257.311.

21 *WCA.* xviii.

22 *VCH Oxon,* xii, 401.

23 *VCH Oxon,* xii, 440.

24 ORO MSS. Wills (Oxon), 153/3/50.

25 *VCH Oxon,* xii, 31.

26 Marshall, 208.

27 WBM B78/2 and 3.

28 WBM B78/2 *f 128v.*

29 *WCA,* 111.

30 WBM B78/3 *f 44v.*

31 *WCA,* 105.

32 ORO MSS. Wills (Oxon), 18/1/1.

33 *WCA,* 237.

34 ORO MSS. Wills (Oxon), 71/2/35.

35 Marshall 208.

36 *VCH Oxon,* xii, 329.

37 Marshall, 225.

38 Tyzack C., *Wychwood and Cornbury,* Wychwood Press (2003) 65.

39 London Marriage Licences, 1611-1828, (Harleian Soc., vol.ii, 236).

40 PRO PROB 11/290.

41 *VCH Oxon,* xii, 401.

42 *VCH Oxon,* xii, 440.

43 Black Bourton registers.

44 PRO PROB 11/365.

45 ORO Berks and Oxon Marriage Bonds index.

46 An officer who buys provisiions for colleges etc. OED

47 J Shipp, *Accounts of William Whitton* unpub.1993.

48 *VCH Oxon,* xii, 332.

49 *VCH Oxon,* xii, 460.

50 *VCH Oxon,* xii, 448.

Appendix

Oxfordshire Record Office – Probate documents

297/2/36	FLETCHER, Joseph	1661	Accounts
179:66	FLETCHER, Thomas	1545	Will
179:166	GLOVER, John	1546	Will
183:310	GLOVER, John	1559	Will
297/3/61	GLOVER, John	1643	Inventory
166/4/9	GLOVER, Michael	1725	Will and Inventory
80/1/30	GLOVER, Nicholas	1620	Administration
27/4/23	GLOVER, Thomas	1683	Will and Inventory
186:77	GLOVER, William	1579	Administration
131/4/23	HOLLIS, Edith	1632	Will and Inventory
131/4/1	HOLOWAY, John	1585	Will
38/1/18	JOHNSON, Alexander	1680/1	Will and Inventory
137/1/28	JOHNSON, Benjamin	1714	Will and Inventory
38/2/10	JOHNSON, Edmund	1688/9	Will and Inventory
168/3/36	JOHNSON, Joan	1695	Inventory
39/3/1	KEENE, Mary	1626	Will and Inventory
41/2/36	LEAKE, Anne	1613/15	Will and Inventory
139/1/31 107:09	LOVE, Thomas	1628/31	Will, Inventory and Administration
181:34	NASH, John (of Bicester)	1556	Will
183:163	NASH, Margery "	1559	Will
171/1/6	NASH, Thomas	1605	Administration
47/2/40	NASHE, Jerome	1623	Will and Inventory
186:32	NASHE, Michael	1570	Will
185:249	NASHE, William	1574	Will
47/4/23	NICHOLLS, Elizabeth	1648	Will and Inventory
47/4/13	NICHOLLS, James	1640/1	Will and Inventory
47/1/12	NURSE, John	1587	Will
47/2/2	NURSE, Margery	1607	Will and Administration
89/1/16	NURSE, Michael	1609	Administration Bond
47/1/3	NURSE, Richard	1583	Will
47/1/13	NURSE, Robert	1587	Will
50/1/59	PRESTMAN, Thomas	1590	Will
183:54	PYMAN, William	1558	Will
299/7/40	READE, Richard	1647	Inventory and Accounts
147/1/12	REYLEY, John	1589	Will and Inventory
299/7/57	RICHARDSON, Francis	1674	Inventory and Accounts
182:39	SAVAGE, John	1557	Will
62/4/11	SPARROW, Elizabeth	1690/3	Will and Inventory
62/1/9	SPARROW, Thomas	1678	Will and Inventory

65/2/26	TASSELL, Robert	1600	Will and Inventory
178:111	TAYLOR, John	1533	Will
153/3/50	TODMAN, William	1624	Will
71/2/35	WHITTON, John	1642	Will
180:251	WHITTON, Owen	1554	Will
184:379	WILKINSON, Robert	1568	Will
72/4/9	WILLIAMS, Amy	1680	Will and Inventory
156/1/13	WILLIAMS, Katherine	1583	Will
184:44	WILLIAMS, Richard	1562	Will
71/1/21	WILLIAMS, Thomas	1636	Will

Oxfordshire Record Office – Diocesan records

Churchwardens' accounts 1613 to 1702 (Oxon Archives DD Par Woodstock C12)

Registers of baptisms, marriages and burials from the following parishes

Black Bourton

Bladon, including Hensington

New Woodstock

Spelsbury

Wootton, including Old Woodstock

Public Record Office: now National Archives
Wills proved in Prerogative Court of Canterbury (PCC)

PRO Ref	PCC ref.	Name	Year
PROB 11/37	18 Moore	ANDREWS, Richard	1554
PROB 11/375.38		BATHURST, Dorothy	1684
PROB 11/257.311		BLUNT, Nicholas	1656
PROB 11/194/175		BRADSHAW, Mary	1645
PROB 11/137.7	7 Dale	BROWNE, Thomas, senior	1620
PROB 11/145.227	36 Clarke	BROWNE, Thomas, junior	1625
PROB 11/234.74		FLETCHER, Joseph	1654
PROB 11/248.272		GLOVER, Joan	1655
PROB 11/111.20		METCALF, William	1609
PROB 11/84.62	62 Dixy	NASH, Hilary	1594
PROB 11/174.272		NASH, Richard	1637
PROB 11/108	98 Stafford	WHITTON, George	1606
PROB 11/290.211		WHITTON, Gerrard	1659
PROB 11/365.21		WHITTON, Nicholas	1681

Woodstock Borough Muniments now housed in Oxfordshire Record Office

WBM	B78/2	Woodstock Portmoot Court book 1608 to 1613
WBM	B78/3	Woodstock Portmoot Court book 1614 to 1622
WBM	B81	Chamberlains' annual audit 1590 to 1664
WBM	B76	Council Minutes 1661 to 1670
WBM	B96	Inhabitants lists 1611 to 1748
WBM	B82	Constitution of 1580
WBM	B83	Rent Roll 1468/9
WBM	B96	Rent Roll 1598, 1601/2, 1608/9, 1614
WBM	B 7	Rent Roll 1652/3

Published by Oxford Record Society

Vol. 58   Woodstock Chamberlains' Accounts 1609-50   Ed. M. Maslen 1993

Vol. 63   Calendar of the Court Books of the Borough of New Woodstock 1588 –95

Ed. R.F. Taylor 2002

Index of persons

Abbreviations: ald – alderman; bro – brother; dau – daughter; jun – junior; m – married; sen – senior; sis – sister; s – son; w – wife; wid – widow

Dates of death are included as necessary to identify individuals of the same Christian name

George, s John (d.1648), 52, 54, 55, 56, 57, 58, 59
George, s Robert, ald., 52, 58, 59
Henry, cordwainer, s John (d.1648), 52, 55, 56, 57, 59
Hester, w Bartholomew, innkeeper (d.1741), 52, 59
Jane (d.1635), w John (d.1648), 52, 56
Jane (d.1671), dau Robert, ald., 52, 58, 59
Joan, dau Robert, ald., 52, 58
Joan, widow, m John Savage, 52
John Crispin, s Richard, 52
John, (d.1648), s John als. Cowper (d.1602), 20, 32, 52, 53, 54, 55, 56, 57
John, goldsmith, London, 68
John, s John (d.1648), 54, 56
John, s Robert, ald., 52, 57, 58, 59, 86
Marie, dau Henry & Anne, 52, 59
Mary, dau Robert, ald., 52, 58
Mr, 56
Richard Norman, s Richard & Elizabeth, 52
Richard, s Bartholomew & Sarah nee Norman, 52, 59
Robert, ald., s John (d.1648), 20, 52, 56, 57, 58, 59, 86
Robert, s Robert, ald., 52, 58, 59
Samuel, s John (d.1648), 52, 56, 59
Sarah (d.1855), w William, 52, 60
Solomon Flie, 58
Thomas Burborough, 52
Ursula, dau Joan, widow, 52, 53
William, s John (d.1648), 52, 56, 59
William, s Richard & Elizabeth, 52, 60
Cooper als. Cowper
John (d.1602), 20, 28, 52, 53, 54, 55
Cornishe
Elizabeth, nee Browne, w Henry, 46, 49
Henry, 42, 47, 49
John, 42, 47
Sarah, 42, 47
Cornwell
family, 64
Joan, wid John, 64
John, s William, ald., 62, 64
Margaret, nee Fletcher, w Robert, 64
Mary, nee Beston, w Richard (d.1585), m John Doleman, 64
Richard (d.1585), founder of grammar school, 20, 62, 64, 65, 66, 67, 68, 70
Robert, s William, ald., 20, 62, 64
William, ald., 20, 62, 63, 64
Cox
Clemence, nee Nash, 92, 93
John, s Clemence, 92
John, bro Mary Bradshaw (d.1645), 40
John, m — Vernon, 42
Cromwell
Oliver, 18, 112

Damery
Anne, dau John & Anne, 22
Anne, nee Tassell, w John, 22
Elizabeth, dau John & Anne, 22
John, (d.1610), s John & Anne, 22
John, (d.1632), s John & Anne, 22
John, of Bladon, m Anne Tassell, 22, 24
Margaret, dau John & Anne, 22
Mary, dau John & Anne, 22
Michael, s John & Anne, 22
Richard, s John & Anne, 22
Stephen, s John & Anne, 22
Thomas, s John & Anne, 22
William, s John & Anne, 22
Darling
Alice, 104, 108, 111
Davis
Benjamin, s John & Grace nee Johnson, 82, 88, 89
Edmund, s John & Grace nee Johnson, 82, 88
Grace, dau John & Grace nee Johnson, 82, 88
Grace, wid John, m Edward Ryves, 89, 90
John, mercer, m Grace Johnson, 20, 82, 88, 89
Dawks
Elizabeth, m Joseph Fletcher (d.1654), 62, 68
Daysey
George, m Frances Richardson, 101
Dingley
Edulph, 107
Diston
William, 47
Doleman
John, 62, 64
Mary, wid Richard Cornwell, m John, 64
Dubber
Elizabeth, dau Margaret, m Thomas Browne, ald.?, 42, 46
John, s Margaret, 24, 42, 46, 48
Margaret, m (1) — Dubber, (2) Richard Fernsyde, (3) Thomas Prestman, 42, 46
Mary, dau Margaret, 42, 46
Richard, s John, 44
Dunford
William, 84
Durbridge
Ralph, 97

Edwardes
Anne, dau Walter, 22, 23, 24
George, bro Walter, 23, 24
Margaret, wid Robert Tassell, m Walter Edwardes, 22, 23
Walter, m Margaret Tassell, widow, 22, 23, 24